SPSS

FOR APPLIED SCIENCES

To the memory of George Orwell and the quest for objectivity.

SPSS
FOR APPLIED SCIENCES

Basic Statistical Testing

Cole Davis

National Library of Australia Cataloguing-in-Publication entry

Davis, Cole, author.

SPSS for applied sciences : basic statistical testing / Cole Davis.

9780643107106 (paperback)
9780643107113 (epdf)
9780643107120 (epub)

Includes bibliographical references and index.

SPSS (Computer file)
Interactive computer systems
Technology – Computer programs
Problem solving – Statistical methods

005.36

Published by
CSIRO PUBLISHING
36 Gardiner Road, Clayton VIC 3168
Private Bag 10, Clayton South VIC 3169
Australia

Telephone: [+613] 9545 8555
Local call: 1300 788 000 (Australia only)
Fax: +61 3 9662 7555
Email: csiropublishing@csiro.au
Web site: www.publishing.csiro.au

Front cover: image by iStockphoto
Set in Lucida 9/15
Cover design by James Kelly
Text design by Andrew Weatherill
Typeset by Desktop Concepts Pty Ltd, Melbourne
Printed by Ingram Lightning Source

Mar26_RP_ILS

Contents

PART ONE

Pre-test considerations

CHAPTER 1

Introduction

WHAT THIS BOOK DOES

After an introduction which should be invaluable to beginners and those returning to statistical testing after a break, this book introduces statistical tests in a well-organised manner, providing worked examples using both parametric and non-parametric tests.

Whether you are a beginner or an intermediate level test user, you should be able to use this book to analyse different types of data in applied settings. It should also give you the confidence to use other statistical software and to extend your expertise to more specific scientific settings as required.

This book assumes that many applied researchers, scientific or otherwise, will not want to use statistical equations or to learn about a range of arcane statistical concepts. Instead, it is a very practical, easy and speedy introduction to data analysis in the round, offering examples from a range of scenarios from applied science, handling both continuous and rough-hewn data sets.

Examples will be found from agriculture, arboriculture, audiology, biology, computer science, ecology, engineering, epidemiology, farming and farm management, hydrology, medicine, ophthalmology, pharmacology, physiotherapy, spectroscopy and sports science. These disciplines have not been covered in depth, as this book is intended to provide a general approach to solving problems using statistical tests.

The output, with permission from IBM, comes from SPSS (PASW) Student Version 18, for the purpose of the widest usability, and the Advanced Module of SPSS 20. It is completely compatible with SPSS versions 17 to 20 (including those packages with the title PASW) and will generally be usable with earlier editions. As SPSS tends not to change much over the years, this book is likely to be relevant for quite some time. SPSS features are used selectively here for the sake of clarity. Various manuals and handbooks are available on the internet and in print for those eager to know every possible detail of its use.

Similarly, as the book is essentially about statistical testing, research design is generally only touched on for the purposes of clarity. Again, there are a lot of sources of information out there, especially relating to different specialisms.

In contrast to many books on statistics, I favour coherence over conceptual comprehensiveness, although as will be seen, this book offers some tests not usually found in other introductory books.

THE ORGANISATION OF CONTENT

Although many core concepts are presented in the first part of the book, which should definitely be read by newcomers to statistical testing, other ideas appear where they logically arise. Although mathematics is barely touched upon, statistical jargon is introduced, as you will meet it in SPSS and other software as well as in research papers which you may read or even find yourself writing. Descriptive statistics are introduced, as it is important in the preliminary analysis of data, but are dealt with sparingly: inferential statistics are at the heart of statistical testing. The first part of the book also offers a quick and basic guide to using SPSS.

The second part of the book comprises the tests. Each test is accompanied by at least one worked example. Where possible, non-parametric equivalents are provided in addition to parametric tests; we recognise that data sets in the real world are not always as blandly measurable as we would wish them to be.

The chapter on experiments and quasi-experiments – essentially, the analysis of differences – is fairly conventional, apart from equal consideration being given to non-parametric tests as useful tools in applied settings. Factorial analysis of variance (e.g. two-way ANOVA) is also covered, although a discussion about the analysis of covariance (ANCOVA) is deferred until the brief chapter on advanced techniques.

The chapter on the frequency of observation – also known as qualitative (or categorical) analysis – offers a broader set of practical usages than in most introductory texts.

Survival analysis is also new to general introductory texts, but given its wide applicability outside the world of medicine, I prefer to call it the analysis of the time until events. Although this is also qualitative in nature, it is so different in function as to be worthy of a separate chapter.

The next chapter starts with correlations, but goes beyond some contemporary texts in introducing multiple regression, which is increasingly used in applied settings. It also provides a stripped down account of factor analysis, which will meet the needs of people on master's and doctoral projects (and others) who find themselves needing to use this technique in a hurry. Many so-called simple introductions are generally nothing of the sort. The core coverage provided here meets immediate needs, but will also make it easier to absorb more in-depth texts when necessary.

The third part of the book includes a short set of exercises. Problems in the real world are not usually accompanied by signposts saying 'this problem involves correlations', so I have avoided the common practice of putting a quiz at the end of each chapter. I think it makes most sense to tackle exercises once you have an overall grasp of what you have read and the experience of having worked through the preceding worked examples.

The chapter on reporting is intended for organisations with practical concerns; academic writers will need to use works of reference specific to their disciplines or universities. The book concludes with a brief summary of a few advanced statistical techniques.

DATA SETS AND ADDITIONAL INFORMATION

The data sets are small, to avoid lengthy data entry or the need for internet downloads. Following the same logic, some data sets are built upon as each chapter progresses. While the worked examples should be of interest to various practitioners, it should be noted that the data sets are for learning purposes only and are fictional unless there is a clear statement to the contrary.

The book contains various 'discussion points', which draw the reader's attention to statistical topics that are philosophically interesting or controversial.

On the subject of controversy, I may add that independent researchers will find SPSS to be rather an expensive piece of software. A cheaper option is StatsDirect. I wrote a book to accompany this package (Davis 2010), but do note that the data sets and texts are similar in both books. I do not recommend buying both. If a choice has to be made, then this book is more comprehensive in its range of tests and concepts.

HOW TO USE THIS BOOK

If you do not have to time to read the whole book, it is still a good idea to read the introductory part before homing in on the chapter of interest. If time dictates dipping into a single chapter, then try to read the whole chapter and follow the worked examples.

References to statistical theory may be skipped over by first time readers, but they may in time improve your understanding of the issues. When you have a full grasp of this book, you should be able to use other software and more advanced tests.

ACKNOWLEDGEMENTS

I would particularly like to thank Dr George Clegg, a scientist with experience in academic research and the defence industry, who asked some hard questions about what I intended to write. Thanks are also due to Nick Jones for his encouragement during the development of this book, and Ofra Reuven, statistician and data analyst, for her speedy and reliable help creating images and checking through my data.

Permission was granted by IBM to use screenshots from the IBM statistical testing package.

I would also like to thank the Orwell Estate for their goodwill over the dedication of this book. George Orwell's essays and books have given me food for thought and themes for debate over the decades. His integrity stands as a beacon.

The responsibility for any shortcomings remains my own.

DISCUSSION POINT

Statistical testing is like driving a car. You need to know where you are going and what to do when you get there, but the workings of the engine need not necessarily bother you. It is my contention that formulae are of little relevance to effective data analysis.

CHAPTER 2

Descriptive and inferential statistics introduced

DESCRIPTIVE STATISTICS

This book is primarily about inferential statistics, generalising from limited data, but some knowledge of descriptive statistics is essential. When we have all the data, the entire population rather than a sample, descriptive statistics may tell us all we need to know. When looking at samples, the descriptive data helps us to decide which statistical tests to use and indeed if any tests should be used. The statistical concepts discussed (lightly) here underlie what the tests try to achieve.

A **statistic** is a number which represents or summarises data. Descriptive statistics reveal how much data is involved and its **shape**.

There are times when an absolute number gives us what we want. We can have 99 red balloons, 20 000 drug addicts and 101 Dalmatians. There are also simple representative statistics such as the **range**, the maximum minus the minimum: if the maximum is 206 and the minimum is 186, then the range statistic is 20.

Measures of central tendency

When we contrast groups of data, we run into the limitations of absolute numbers. For example, the comparison of the effects of alcohol intake between individuals may be misleading if we do not take into account the size of the individual. Therefore, we tend to use central tendency as one of the ways to reduce irrelevant differences.

The measure of central tendency is also sometimes referred to as the 'average'. However, the term average is problematic in more than one way.

Part of the problem is that of interpretation. We can see the dubious nature of the layman's 'average' when we consider newspaper articles that refer to 'average pay'. I do not know which average is being referred to – the mean, the mode or the median – and it is likely that the journalist is similarly unsure. A related problem is that the word 'average' is associated by many with just one particular measure of central tendency, the mean. This being the case, 'central tendency' is to be preferred when referring to statistical principles. (However, there are times when 'average' slips more easily from the tongue, pen or keyboard.)

THE MEAN

The mean adds the numbers in the data set and divides the sum by the number of items, as in this simple example: **2, 3, 3, 4, 8**. The sum, Σ, = 20. The number of items, N, = 5. The mean is therefore Σ / N: 20/5 = 4.

If we use the mean to calculate the central tendency in workers' salaries, the strength of this method is that it takes into account everyone from multimillionaires to the lowest paid. This is also its weakness, as the presence of one or two billionaires could provide a highly unrepresentative statistic.

THE MODE

The mode is the number which appears most frequently in a data set, in this case the number 3.

The mode will successfully ignore the presence of our uber-tycoons, as most salary earners may well be clerical workers. But how representative is this of the earnings of the workforce in general?

THE MEDIAN

The median is the value in the middle of the string of numbers on a continuum from biggest to smallest. We count inwards from our tiny data set, discounting first the 2 and the 8, then the outer 3 and the 4, leaving the central 3 in the middle as the median.

In our industrial example, the median statistic may find a middle-manager's salary. This could also be useful, but it does not render the most common wage, for which we need the mode, nor does it take into account the purchasing power of the extremely rich and the extremely poor, as the mean does.

Apart from demonstrating the importance of central tendency as a concept, this shows how interpretative statistical research can be (and I do not mean this in the cynical sense). The context may determine our use of different statistics.

The distribution of data

Central tendency is just part of what is known as the distribution of data, which can be shown using a histogram. Again, we use 2, 3, 3, 4, 8. Techniques such as histograms, as well as simple quantitative statistics such as measures of central tendency, allow us to consider the *shape* of a distribution and hence which type of distribution we are looking at.

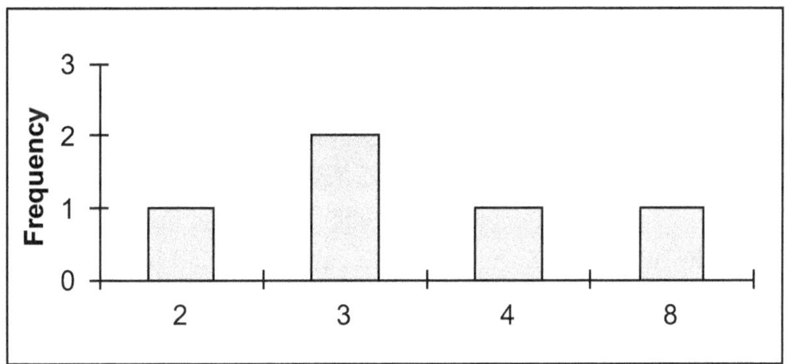

A common distribution is the 'normal distribution', otherwise known as Gaussian distribution, the famous bell curve (an idealised symmetrical one is shown below). This generally represents a natural population, for example, animal running speeds or intelligence test results.

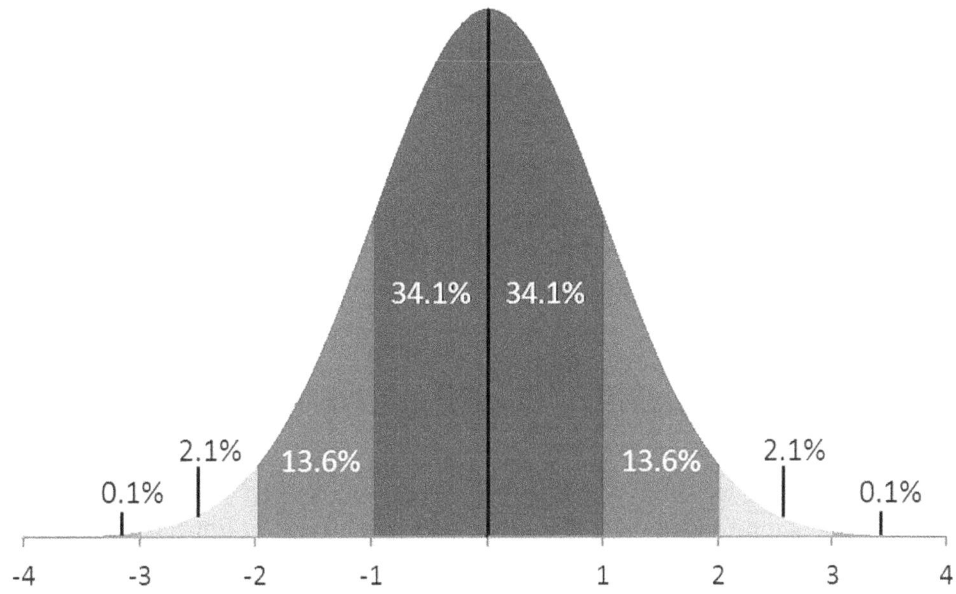

The chart shows some new figures. We already know about the measures of central tendency, the mean, median and mode. However, people can be misled by figures such as the mean, which can be large or small without telling us very much, similarly the median. (The mode has another little foible: it may not be unique, as there may be two or more figures which come up particularly frequently.) So we are also interested in measures of *dispersion*, how spread out the numbers are around the mean.

The figures underneath the chart, running from –4 to +4 represent one measure of dispersion, the *standard deviation*. You will often read reports citing the standard deviation (SD) as well as the mean. As you will see, one standard deviation around the mean (the centre) represents over 68% of the data. Two standard deviations either way represent over 95%, with three SD amounting to 99.6%. Before getting too carried away with the standard deviation, do note that it is not robust when dealing with abnormally distributed data, particularly when it comes to outlying data ('outliers').

Mathematically, the standard deviation is derived from the *variance*, something which will be mentioned occasionally because of its key role in parametric testing.

Another measure of dispersion is the *range*, the difference between the maximum and minimum values. Yet another is the *interquartile range*: just as the median can be used as the central value, dividing the data in half, then the data can be divided into quarters, adding the upper and lower quartiles. This gives the idea of the 'mainstream' values of the data by describing the middle 50% of the distribution without the extremely high or low values.

Returning to normal distribution, it should be noted that the curve can be sharper or more rotund than the one portrayed in our chart while still retaining an even distribution. Such a shape would still be considered 'normal'. However, if the data is not evenly distributed, with a long tail to one side, the distribution is considered to be *skewed*; the data is not normally distributed and would not be suitable for parametric testing, which will be discussed in the next chapter.

Although you may at some time in your statistical career consider binomial, Poisson and even random distributions, this book generally concerns itself with the existence or otherwise of a normal distribution. Having a normal distribution is a major requirement for choosing a parametric test (to be discussed in the next chapter). The relevant measure of central tendency for the statistical testing of parametric data is the mean.

Non-normality may be characterised by peaks occurring way off centre to the left or right. Such 'skewed' data will generally require non-parametric tests. The relevant measure of central tendency for the statistical testing of non-parametric data is the median.

It is also possible to get bimodal distribution, the occurrence of double peaks, which represent two modes. This suggests that there are two data samples or that there are some very peculiar effects. In this case, a careful examination of the data would be in order, but immediate statistical testing would not be advisable.

Similarly, when using measurement-based tests (as opposed to ones examining the frequency of observations or the time between events), we would need to check for linearity, that data follows a straight line. This is discussed in more depth in the chapter on correlations.

When we use both parametric and non-parametric tests, an important concept is that of **variance**. Variability of data around the central tendency can be the effect under examination although, as will be seen, other factors may be responsible. When analysing normally distributed continuous data, we are more likely to use the mean as our measure of central tendency. The median would be more suitable for non-normal continuous data.

INFERENTIAL STATISTICS

When people infer, they can be said to jump to conclusions. Here, we wish to examine data logically and come to *reasonable* conclusions. This is at the heart of statistical testing. Please bear with me while learning some key concepts. We will be getting more practical quite soon.

Samples

Samples are taken from a wider population. The population may comprise the total number of people in a town or country, but in research terms it often refers to a group of interest to us, or target group. This could be mammals or rocks, or more narrowly, mice or basalt.

Given the impracticality of observing most populations as a whole, we usually limit ourselves to samples from the target population. These could comprise, for example, badgers from a selection of districts in a particular region. In some circumstances, samples may be even more restrictive.

Various strategies have been proposed to ensure that sample sizes are representative of a population. One useful idea is to consult the research history relevant to your area of study in order to find similar projects, following the sample sizes previously used. Another is to use published tables; for example, when conducting surveys with calibrated ratings, you may decide to adopt a social science method, choosing sample sizes of between about 30 and 500, the latter figure representing a population of millions (Roscoe 1975).

It should be noted, however, that the size of the population is not necessarily the arbiter of what is a suitable sample size. The variability of the population is important, although larger samples are likely to reduce such variability. On the other hand, the comparative lack of variability in simple, tightly controlled studies (e.g. matching pairs of participants) can mean samples as small as 10 to 20 participants.

There are some more technical methods for estimating sample size, taking into account such concepts as precision, confidence, variability and response rate; however, as you will see if you use internet calculators to work out suitable samples (e.g. Raosoft 2004), subjective decisions are still to be made at every turn.

There are some general rules of thumb for certain circumstances. When samples are broken down into sub-samples (e.g. males/females), the sub-samples generally require at least 30 participants per category. Multivariate techniques and multiple regression require sample sizes several times bigger than the number of variables (variables are discussed when we get to the chapter on experiments and quasi-experiments), preferably 10 times as many. Smaller samples may be used, but it must be recognised that there are dangers in being rather unrepresentative and also that real (if small) effects may be missed. (The samples used in this book are deliberately small and artificial.)

In search of an effect

Assuming reliable measurement, descriptive statistics would be sufficient to describe a perceived phenomenon within an entire population. The perceived phenomenon is known as the **effect**.

When inferring from a sample, however, we cannot be sure how representative it is of the population from which it is drawn. The reason for using statistical tests, at least at this introductory level, is to calculate the likely existence or otherwise of an effect from a sample of data. Essentially, we want to know if there are real differences (or, with correlations, relationships) between two or more sets of data. Again, these are effects.

Significance

This section deals with '*p* values', 'null hypotheses' and 'alternative hypotheses'. Whether or not these terms are new to you, it is recommended that you read this section carefully.

Note that I recently referred to *real* differences or relationships between data. With any samples, we cannot be sure about the meaningfulness or otherwise of an effect. The perceived effect could be a chance fluctuation in the data or the impact of a different, perhaps unexpected, effect.

The point of **significance testing** is to decide whether or not the perceived phenomenon is a fluke. Let us say, for example, that the same sample of people have their glucose levels tested in the morning and the evening. We want to know if the time of day matters. Having said that, extraneous factors such as differing food intake, experiences at a given time, or the onset of illness, could also affect results. Assuming we have taken reasonable precautions relating to these other factors, we hope that the use of statistics here would be to see if there is a significant difference between glucose levels at these times.

The **null hypothesis**, beloved of many an academic author, states that any perceived effect is, in fact, a matter of chance or a non-relevant factor. If, in our example, any differences in glucose level are likely to be down to meal portions of unusual size or carbohydrate level, then *the null hypothesis is accepted.* In everyday terms, the result is *not significant.*

If, however, there is a clear difference between glucose levels in the morning and the evening, then academically speaking, *the null hypothesis is rejected*, or *the alternative hypothesis* (the alternative to chance fluctuation) *is accepted.* In everyday terms, the result is *significant.*

These definitions will be encountered frequently in text books, academic reporting and in statistical software packages. When reporting in applied research, however, and for your own sanity, a result caused by chance or an interfering factor, can simply be referred to as *not significant.* The 'real' effect can be referred to as a *significant* effect or result.

You may wonder why I have discussed non-significance (the null hypothesis) first and only then the sought after significant result. Well, tests of significance are concerned with the likelihood of an effect being the result of extraneous factors, the existence of the null hypothesis. They calculate the variance, and like the computers running them, they do not share your enthusiasm for significant effects; they are designed to detect the *probability of a chance result.*

This book does not concern itself with calculations of probability. We consider merely the question, 'is the effect significant or a matter of irrelevant fluctuation?'

Which takes us to the ***p* value**. The *p* value of a test is the measure of significance, *the likelihood of a result being insignificant.*

The percentage of the *p* value is the calculated chance of your getting a fluke test result. A *p* value of .03, for example, means that there is a three in a hundred chance that the result has emerged from irrelevant fluctuations. Your result is likely to be significant.

Please do not start talking about 97% success rates or the like. Stick with .03, which tells you that, according to the statistical calculations, if you tried the test on a hundred samples, there would be a 3% chance of a fluke result. It looks good, but your result could still be that three-in-a-hundred irrelevance.

This leads to a very common research problem. In general terms if you run a battery of tests, 'dredging' for significant results being a common temptation, there is a greatly increased chance of some fluke results. (A false positive is known as a Type 1 error. A Type 2 error, by the way, is a false negative, where you miss what is in fact a significant finding.)

This is why replication of results is often recommended. (The issue of 'reliability' appears occasionally in this book, but the reader may profit from more in-depth discussions in books about research in general.)

The highest *p* value is 1. A *p* value such as .337 suggests a random or irrelevant fluctuation. The value .333 informs us that there is a one in three chance of the result being a fluke. The result could be replicated, but it probably is not worth doing. But what level of significance is worth considering?

An alternative to the *p* value is the **critical value**: *p* is smaller than something. Commonly quoted critical values are $p < 0.05$, $p < 0.01$ and $p < 0.001$. The chances of a fluke result are calculated respectively as being less than five in a hundred (5%), less than one in a hundred and less than one in a thousand. Other critical values sometimes used are $p < .02$ and $p < .005$. All refer to the likelihood of any variance being a matter of chance or unexpected factors.

Although it is quite common to merely 'read off' the *p* values or critical values from the computerised results, some would argue that the researcher should decide upon an acceptable level of significance *before* using the statistical tests, determining an acceptable level of risk or academic rigour. While $p < .05$ may be acceptable for a small sample involving a group of biology students, with replication being a matter for next year, a more definitive research project may want the chance of an error to be less than $p < .01$. An aircraft manufacturer may want $p < .0001$, with replications. If the result is 'read off' the computer, then we are not basing our analysis on acceptable risk to the organisation involved.

Not everybody agrees with this approach. Another view is that the *p* value by itself allows people to draw their own conclusions. If the test comes out with .03, you may choose to read it as significant at $p < .05$, while another reader of the report who believes $p < .01$ to be more suitable may view the result as non-significant. Indeed, if you only report the chosen critical value, e.g. $p < .05$, without offering the *p* value, the reader would be unable to do this. To satisfy both viewpoints, the answer is to cite both the critical value that you originally set (e.g. $p < .01$) and also the *p* value itself, e.g. '$p = .03$; not significant at $p < .01$'.

A final point when deciding upon an acceptable level of significance is the question of **one-tailed** and **two-tailed** hypotheses. A one-tailed hypothesis means that the direction is theoretically clear to you from the outset. You expect the result to go in a particular direction. A two-tailed hypothesis means that you cannot be sure in which direction a significant result would run. (These terms refer respectively to variance from the mean to only one end of the distribution versus possible variance either way.) For example, if you are already sure that the glucose levels are higher in mornings than in evenings and have good reasons for this being the case (and this is confirmed by the test), and the statistical test indicated that $p < .01$, you could accept that there is less than a 1% chance of a fluke result. If, however, you have not been committed in terms of the direction of the effect, a chance result is twice as likely (there is variance to either side of the mean). So you double the critical value, declaring the result to be a more rigorous $p < .02$ two-tailed. You are a little less sure about the likelihood of significance; instead of a 1% chance of a fluke, you concede a 2% possibility.

If it helps, here is a pictorial representation of one- and two-tailed hypotheses (the numbers underneath represent standard deviations from the mean).

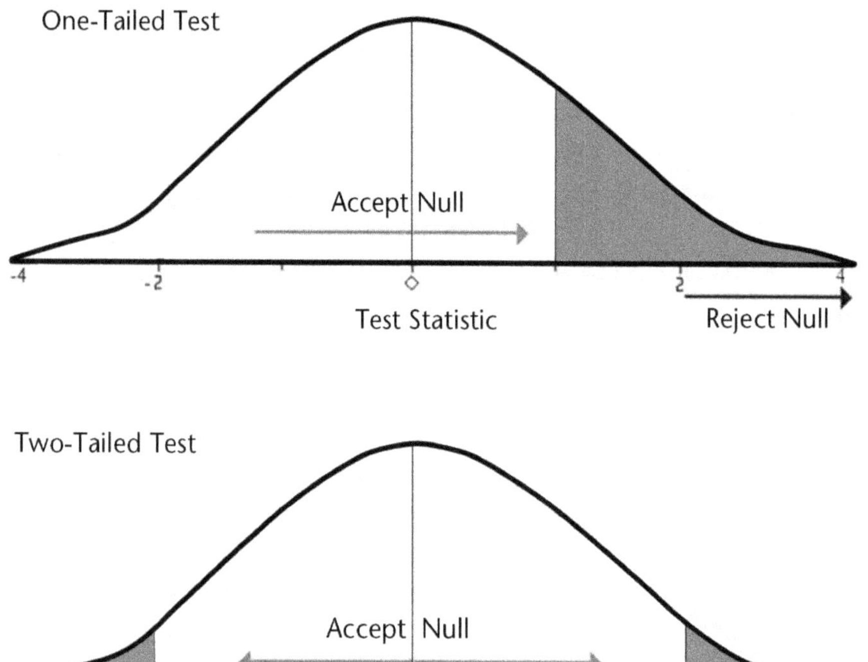

In academic reporting, you would refer to the result being 'significant at $p < .01$ one-tailed' or 'significant at $p < .02$ two-tailed'. In non-academic reports, you would just quote the level of significance as being $p < .01$ or $p < .02$.

Effect size

While significance refers to the likelihood of an effect's existence, effect size measures the distance of the swing away from the mean, the variance. One may come across results of quite high significance but relatively low effect size. In such cases, the effect only contributes very little to the variance. Maybe other effects are at large, or there is experimental 'noise', random factors introduced into the environment. In practical terms, we can be fairly sure of an effect's existence, but it may not always be of much practical relevance.

In SPSS, you will meet various effect size statistics, especially r^2 and Partial Eta Squared. SPSS will not make it clear if an effect is large, small or middling in size, so value judgements have to be made. Looking at the findings of previous similar research is particularly recommended. However, if in doubt, rules of thumb are provided in various sections of the book.

DISCUSSION POINT

Books on statistics and statistical software churn out all manner of statistics. One example is kurtosis, which represents the flatness of the distribution curve. You are unlikely ever to use this in your research. The author never has.

Another point: sometimes descriptive statistics are all you need. If you already have the data for a whole population, you don't need to infer: a population is already representative of itself.

Inferential statistics should be used when there is something you want to infer from the data. This may be when you only have a sample from the population, but can also be to compare (or contrast) one part of the population with another. The subgroups may differ in more ways than just the measure in which you are interested, so the test can to some extent allow for fluctuations.

CHAPTER 3

Parametric and non-parametric tests

DIFFERENT TYPES OF DATA

An important issue in quantitative research is that of the 'criterion problem'. The criterion is what is measured. If this is irrelevant or inappropriate for the test being used, then no estimations of significance can be considered valid; we have built on a house of cards. The accuracy of measurement, and reliability in general, is a matter of research design and is not therefore our primary concern in this book, but the issue of data being appropriate for running particular tests must be discussed.

Different tests carry different assumptions about the data under analysis. The assumptions that concern us most regularly in this book are the ones leading to the decision about whether or not we can use parametric tests.

Running tests with inappropriate data can lead to a mass of apparently significant (or insignificant) results which are, in fact, meaningless. This sort of error is easily made and computer software packages will often be as unaware of the problem as you are. So data should be examined before you use parametric tests, including using descriptive statistics. You must ensure that the data you input is appropriate. In most cases, this includes using the same type of numbers in all variables used.

One way of conceptualising the different types of data is to consider its texture. Is it finely chopped or coarse? Here, I want to look at three types of measurement data: continuous, ordinal and categorical.

At the fine end, we have **continuous** data (referred to as **Scale** by SPSS). This exists as an apparently 'natural' run of information. Distances, seconds and ages (where they are not banded) are of this kind. Continuous data may be subdivided into ratio data and interval data. Ratio data runs from zero (e.g. 0, 1 second, 2 seconds, etc.), while interval data can start with a higher number (as in running speeds: 10 km/h, 11 km/h, etc.). Statistical tests in this book do not differentiate between ratio and interval types. In general terms, continuous data are usually the grist for parametric tests. These use the mean, which should also be cited when providing descriptive statistics.

At times, you may be unsure as to whether or not you are dealing with truly continuous data. Ask yourself if doubling or halving a given amount will give a meaningful result. If it does, it is truly continuous.

IQ results appear to be continuous data, but is somebody with an IQ of 140 exactly twice as intelligent as somebody tested as having an IQ of 70? Similarly, the idea of doubling or halving a Likert scale rating from a questionnaire (see below) is a dubious one:

Table 3.1

1	2	3	4	5	6
Very unsatisfied	Unsatisfied	Indifferent	Satisfied	Very satisfied	Ecstatic

Ordinal data is so-called because it can be ordered, or ranked, even though they are not 'smooth' and are not subject to the same arithmetical manipulation as continuous numbers. Such 'lumpy data' – e.g. 3, 13, 23, 25, 60, 80 – are generally examined by non-parametric tests (see below), which puts them into a rank order of magnitude. The median is the measure of central tendency which should be cited from descriptive statistics.

At the far end of our data continuum is **categorical** data, otherwise known as **nominal** (in SPSS Variable View) or **qualitative** data. These numbers are like 'elephants and telegraph poles', entities which do not mix. *Each category must be exclusive: each observation is counted up to make the* **frequency** *within one category.*

Categorical data can be **dichotomous** (male/female, yes/no, etc.). It can also include arbitrary classifications created by the researcher. Examples could include types of rock (igneous, sedimentary, metamorphic), people exhibiting different behaviours (washes hands consistently, washes sporadically, washes rarely or never) or agglomerations of ranges of numbers (heavy, middling, light).

This qualitative choice raises a fundamental research consideration. There should be a theory behind a decision to test for significance. This does not have to be an academic theory, but some form of rationale should justify your decision to test. Otherwise, you may be doing the equivalent of just putting data into the computer and hoping that what emerges is meaningful – which it probably won't be.

(Mixed data, including dichotomous, or binary data, can be subjected to logistic regression, but that takes us outside this introductory volume.)

PARAMETRIC VERSUS NON-PARAMETRIC DATA

In most cases in this book, you will find that there is a choice between using parametric and non-parametric tests.

Parametric tests can be used when certain **assumptions** are made about the parameters (the limits and nature) of the data. Data should be *continuous* (i.e. naturally proportioned), should form a *normal distribution*, and if the samples are of unequal size, should contain *homogeneity of variance*. Essentially, homogeneity of variance means that numbers in the data sets should be of the same proportion (*not*, for example, 2, 3, 4, 5, 3 tested against 23, 28, 33, 46, 30, 43).

As a rule of thumb, experimental and quasi-experimental data, when continuous, may be suitable for parametric tests. Tests which look for normal distribution include the Shapiro–Wilk test for sample sizes of less than 50 and Kolmogorov–Smirnov for larger samples.

If parametric assumptions are not met, you should use a **non-parametric test**. Consider the numbers 16, 15, 13, 32, 4, 4 and 3.

A parametric test, which works using the mean as its measure of central tendency, would certainly be much affected by the far-flung number 32. A non-parametric test would rank the data like so:

* 32 (1st), 16 (2nd), 15 (3rd), 13 (4th), 4 (5th equal), 4 (5th equal), 3 (7th). The largest number is just another number, with no influence beyond its ranking.

As usual when using statistical tests, check your descriptive statistics first. Is the outlier (32, in this case) a legitimate part of your data set? If it is a matter of poor data entry, it is appropriate to alter this without commentary. If you decide that this was an uncharacteristic performance, you may consider ignoring the record when analysing the data by treating it as a 'missing value' (although such a decision should be carefully considered and recorded). If the outlier is legitimate, a non-parametric test can use the data without being unduly influenced by the extreme fluctuation.

DISCUSSION POINT

Many books recommend the use of parametric tests wherever possible. Parametric tests are considered to be 'more powerful' than their non-parametric alternatives, sensitive enough to detect significant results which may otherwise be missed. The choice, however, is highly dependent upon conditions. As many data analysis conditions in everyday research are not text-book examples, non-parametric tests are more likely to be used. In any case, when confronted with data suitable for parametric tests, non-parametric tests generally produce very similar results.

CHAPTER 4

Using SPSS

DATA ENTRY IN SPREADSHEET FORMATS

For the sake of simplicity, let us use two small sets of numbers:

* 40, 30, 45, 60, 45
* 50, 40, 45, 50, 43.

In spreadsheets, they go into two adjacent columns and this would happen both when the two data sets referred to the same cases or to different cases in each data set.

DATA ENTRY WITH SPSS

With the SPSS structure, adjacent columns are only used when the cases are the same for each column. In other words, these are the same subjects in different conditions.

When the subjects of each data set are different from each other, a different input structure is required in SPSS.

When using SPSS, variables should be named first. For learning purposes, however, we will start entering the scores immediately.

If the cases are the same (within-subjects), we require adjacent score columns. Here, we see five cases, each with two sets of scores.

Table 4.1

1	40	50
2	30	40
3	45	45
4	60	50
5	45	43

Where the cases are different on all occasions (between-subjects), the scores must be in the same column. **In SPSS, each row represents just one case.**

Table 4.2

1	40	1
2	30	1
3	45	1
4	60	1
5	45	1
6	50	2
7	40	2
8	45	2
9	50	2
10	43	2

We now have 10 different cases. The two conditions are entered as categories in the column on the right. Each category represents what SPSS refers to as a **grouping variable**, e.g. Group A = 1, Group B = 2.

Both of these examples include a running total of cases on the left. When you manipulate larger data sets, this tracking allows you to monitor what you are doing.

Variable View

Information is entered into the SPSS **Data Editor**. In practice, you should start by creating the variables in **Variable View**, which is available via a toggle tab at the bottom of the program. It is too easy just to enter columns of numbers in the belief that you will remember what they represent; in the case of any developing project, you will almost inevitably forget and run the risk of putting data in the wrong columns. Variables first!

In Variable View, the variables are shown in columns. The column heading 'Name' on the left is the variable's working name.

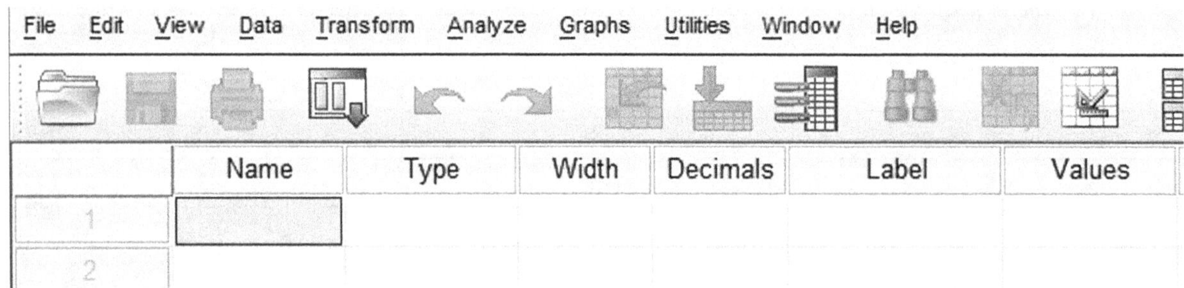

With both of the above data sets, you would first enter under Name something like 'Case'. Each 'Name' is an abbreviation, without gaps between words; this appears in your data column in Data View but does not appear in the SPSS output. (Its full name, which you enter under 'Label', could be something like 'Case number'.)

In the Within-subjects example, the next variable is entered on the next row down (here, I use 'A'), with the other variable ('B') below it. So Variable View will look as follows (the other column settings are defaults):

	Name	Type	Width	Decimals	Label	Values	Missing	Columns	Align	Measure
1	Case	Numeric	8	2		None	None	8	Right	Scale
2	A	Numeric	8	2		None	None	8	Right	Scale
3	B	Numeric	8	2		None	None	8	Right	Scale

Data View | Variable View

It is suggested that you save this file with a name such as 'Same'. We will enter the data shortly.

In the between-subjects example, the second row would be called Score or Result. The next row, here 'Condition', is the grouping variable. The changes to the columns called Decimals, Label and Values will become clearer shortly. Please save this file as something like 'Different'.

	Name	Type	Width	Decimals	Label	Values	Missing	Columns	Align	Measure
1	Case	Numeric	8	0	Case number	None	None	8	Right	Scale
2	Score	Numeric	8	0	Density score	None	None	8	Right	Scale
3	Condition	Numeric	8	0	Iron status	{1, ferrous}...	None	8	Right	Scale

The next column in Variable View is **Type**. This is preset to numeric values but can be set to string (for names) or to settings such as date and currency. The numeric values are pre-set at 2 decimal places, which may become irritating when dealing with integers, so you will frequently set this to zero by clicking on the dots to the right of the relevant cell. If your output is going to use currency other than dollars, you need to go to the menu at the top and find *Edit/Options/Currency*. Here you can define a prefix or suffix (e.g. GBP) which again can be activated by clicking on the cell dots.

Width refers to the column width in Data View, the default being 8. As with the next column, this can be set in the Type column.

Decimals may often be set to zero, to avoid integers with unnecessary retinues (1.00, 2.00, 3.00 ...).

Label is the variable's full name, which will appear in your output. This can contain gaps and should be well-named to aid memory and ease of understanding.

Values are used with *grouping variables*. Each time, you match a code number with a condition name. To do this, click the dots to the right of the cell to reach a dialog box. Let us say that our measurements relate to metals, but that it is important to differentiate between those containing iron and those without. As our condition variable is 'Iron status', you could add 1 to the *value* field in the dialog box and 'ferrous' in the *label* field,

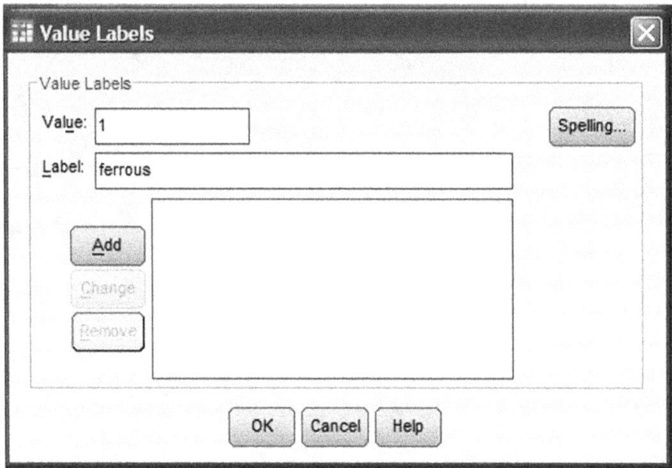

then press 'Add'.

Do the same with 2 and 'non-ferrous', which should give you this:

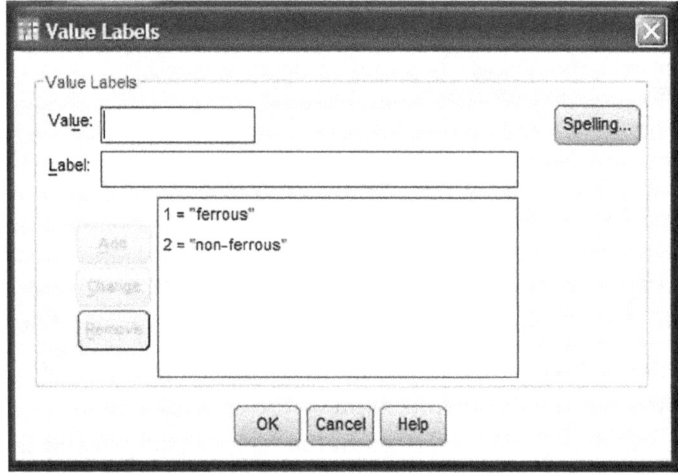

When you are finished, press 'OK'.

The output from any analysis will provide the names of the grouping variables instead of the original numeric values.

Missing – Although SPSS allows for missing values in its calculations ('system-missing values'), you may decide to ignore some values ('user-missing values'). You can specify user-missing values by allocating a number such as –9.

Columns – The width of columns you can see when in Data View.

Align – Cells may be aligned *Left*, *Right* and *Center*. The defaults are right for numbers and left for letter strings.

Measure – 'Scale' is the numerical default, although 'ordinal' is available, as is 'nominal'. Nominal would be used in the case of strings (words), which is necessary when using SPSS charts.

Role – This appears in more recent SPSS editions and relates to task automation in some procedures. 'Input' classifies the variable as an independent variable or predictor (the distinction between these two terms is discussed in the chapter on experimental testing). 'Output' is for a dependent variable or criterion. Also available is a 'Both' option. 'Role' only sets defaults on some dialog boxes and is not essential.

Data View

Again, this is accessible via a toggle tab at the bottom of the program.

If you have already created variables in Variable View, then these should appear at the top of the columns when you move to Data View.

Using the 'Same' file, enter the data from the first data set.

	Case	A	B	var
1	.	40.00	50.00	
2	.	30.00	40.00	
3	.	45.00	45.00	
4	.	60.00	50.00	
5	.	45.00	43.00	
6				
7				
8				
9				
10				
11				
12				

Data View Variable View

To get rid of those annoying zeroes, return to Variable View and adjust the decimals for A and B to zero. Then save the 'Same' file.

Now, on the 'Different' file, enter the scores and grouping variables, then save.

	Case	Score	Condition
1	.	40	1
2	.	30	1
3	.	45	1
4	.	60	1
5	.	45	1
6	.	50	2
7	.	40	2
8	.	45	2
9	.	50	2
10	.	43	2

Data View | Variable View

At the moment, you can see the numbers 1 and 2 entered. If you go to the menu and press on *View/Value Labels*, you will see these converted to 'ferrous' and 'non-ferrous'. A return to the same menu item will toggle off again to the original values.

Note that I have not suggested typing in the case numbers. This is because with large data sets you will almost certainly wish to automate these.

To automate case numbers, ensure that the scores for the relevant variables already exist in Data View and then highlight the empty Case column, as in the image above. Then in Variable View, adjust the variable Case to Decimals = 0 and ensure that 'Case number' is entered in the Label column. Select *Transform/Compute Variable*, typing the word 'Case' into the Target Variable box on the top left. An icon 'Type and Label' will appear underneath; select this and type 'Case number' and press 'Continue'. Then in the main Compute Variable dialog box, type '$CASENUM' into the Numeric Expression field and then press 'OK'.

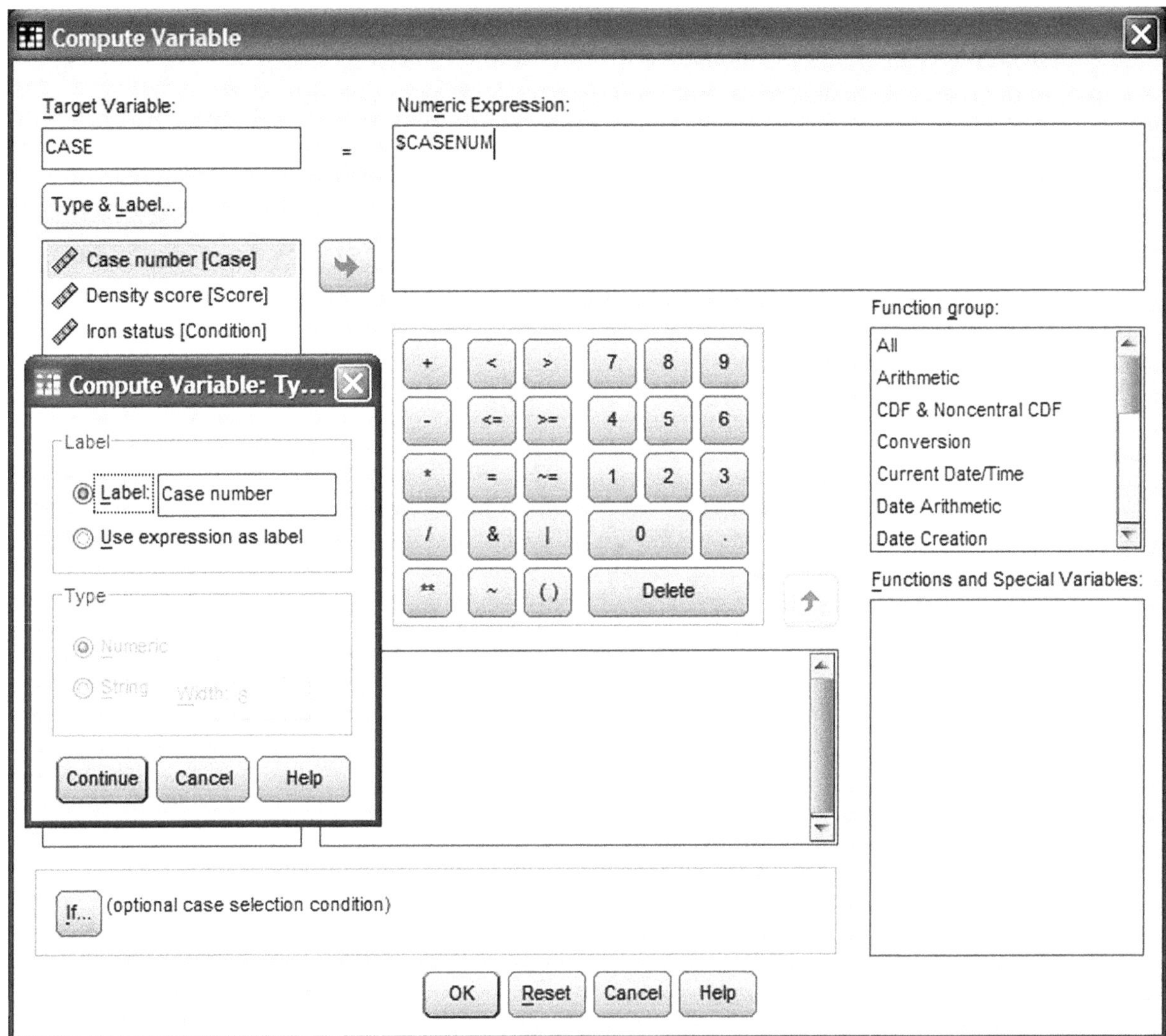

At the moment, Iron status has a 'Scale' symbol attached to it. This should be changed, adjusting the 'Measure' variable to Nominal. If there were a range of rankable values – e.g. very heavy, heavy, medium, etc. – then this would be Ordinal.

Back in *Data* View, the running total should be in place.

Note the status bar at the bottom of the program. It may say that the processor is ready or may monitor the progress of a calculation.

DISCUSSION POINT

Get into the habit of creating variables first in Variable View before entering data into Data View. Create meaningful variable names. The clearer they are, the easier your analysis when things get complicated.

File names should also be clear. Use 'save as' to make new files when you have created data subsets. When updating data sets, file names with dates or edition numbers will allow you to roll back in case of errors. Mistakes happen as projects become more advanced; a well-stocked archive may save a lot of valuable time.

Also, remember to save regularly. A system freeze can lose a lot of work.

CHAPTER 5

Practical research

DATA ANALYSIS IN CONTEXT

Be clear about what is to be researched. If you are not, a desire to 'press the button' and view the automated results may take over. Intelligent data analysis should bear in mind the nature of what is being investigated, as will become particularly clear when we discuss factor analysis.

Similarly, research design ought to be clear from the outset. As well as the obvious reason of wanting to focus upon the area of interest, design has a considerable bearing on how data is collected, collated and analysed.

As well as the more widely publicised ethical issues relating to the collection of data, you need to consider how effective your methods are. Many times have I seen researchers having to alter their projects, surprised to find that busy professionals (and almost everybody else) do not want to complete survey questionnaires with 60 questions. Other researchers fail to carry out pilot projects. Pilots almost always discover errors and sometimes reveal neglected paths of investigation.

If you do not get research design correct the first time around, it can affect data analysis. Radical alterations can mean that different data sets have to be rendered compatible, often requiring data transformation. Other problems may include having too much data, with major resource implications.

If researchers collate observational information, or opinions from interviews, with the intention of performing qualitative analysis, they need to agree on what should be subsumed into categories, both on theoretical grounds and for the purposes of analysis.

Clearly, some consideration of data analysis requirements should be made in advance, but the purpose of the research should be the driving force.

NOTES ON RESEARCH DESIGN

As this book is mainly about statistical testing and more specifically with SPSS, it is impracticable to refer to research design in great detail. Each area of scientific endeavour is rather different in its focus and you should be able to find books on research design which deal with your discipline or a related one.

It may be helpful, however, to outline core research design concerns, with some comments upon their effects on data analysis.

One issue is whether or not a design is experimental. For our purposes, it should be noted that **experiments** are often conducted in everyday settings. A manager, for example, can randomly allocate some workers to a training course and can compare their performance with a control group which is not offered training. The training status is a **variable** (also known in SPSS as a **factor**) which has been manipulated by the manager, who must study the effect of the experiment on yardsticks such as performance measures. We are analysing *differences.*

Random allocation of the subjects (human subjects are often called participants), is generally a sign of a true experiment. Experiments can of course be made more rigorous. Pharmaceutical drugs, for example, are generally tested using a double-blind procedure, neither the patient nor the administrator knowing which drug (if any) is being administered. Subjects are often chosen according to whether or not they have prior knowledge, experience or some form of defining attribute.

In many cases, time and resources mean that we have to be less rigorous and conduct **quasi-experiments**. One example is the choice of fixed groups, such as men and women, or in our manager's case, allocating different types of worker to different courses. Each course, or no course at all, is a **condition**; SPSS also refers to this as a **level**, as it is a level of the variable/factor.

There are also occasions where no positive action has occurred at all, but data is examined retrospectively. Perhaps the training courses took place last year and you have decided to examine the available performance data. 'Experimental' and 'control' groups are still available, but you will be examining historical data as if an experiment has taken place.

The good news from a data analysis perspective is that experiments and quasi-experiments are not viewed differently by statistical tests.

Whether an experiment or a quasi-experiment, a major design issue is that of **between-subjects design** versus **within-subjects design** (within subjects is referred to in SPSS as 'repeated measures'). In the former case, the analysis is of different subjects in each condition; in the latter, the same subjects are studied each time.

In many situations, nature decides on the design, with the default often being between subjects. The main advantage of between-subjects design is freedom from 'carry-over' effects such as order effects. Different subjects are less likely to have experience of the trials. On the other hand, this does not free experiments from contamination effects such as different times of day, contextual and maturational factors. Statistical tests do differentiate between the different designs, so account is taken of error variance, but the researcher should try to minimise such effects wherever possible, as the tests can only do so much.

The main disadvantage of the between-subjects design is of course individual differences. Consider large samples to even out differences. Also, consider randomisation techniques, generally to be found in articles and books on research design.

Within-subjects design of course eradicates individual differences, each case being compared with itself under different conditions. However, as well as order effects, this design is often impracticable. For example, the conditions of being male and female are not usually analysable one after the after in the same case.

If we do wish to eradicate individual differences while using different subjects, we could consider the **matched/paired design**. Instead of the same case under different conditions, different cases would be chosen which are similar in the most relevant attribute(s). Animals, for example, could be found with the same age or health condition if these attributes are the ones of greatest relevance to the experiment. In general, apply within-subjects (repeated-measures) statistical tests to paired design.

Comparative design is very different, examining naturally occurring groups. Instead of allocating persons or things to groups, we observe which cases fall within two or more categories, then testing to see if the observed differences in frequencies are significantly different from the values expected under chance conditions.

Unlike experimental design, we do not use measured data, instead counting up the number of observations in each group, the **frequency** of categorical data.

Naturalistic observations may include preferred habitats and genetic predispositions, for example. These can be categorised and counted. Not only may we study differences between categories, but, using the Chi-square test of association, we can also study relationships between variables.

You can also use qualitative analysis for more general research purposes. I used to gather comments from otherwise structured surveys and from interviews, collating similar comments into what I considered to be meaningful categories. Again, I could look at relationships between categories, for example by sub-dividing the attitudinal reactions according to the rank of the respondent.

Although **longitudinal design** effects can be measured by other methods (e.g. 'before and after' studies of measurable data), one highly useful set of techniques comes under the general heading of **'the time until events'**, or **survival analysis**. This also works by keeping a frequency count, but this time of events occurring over time. As will be seen, this can be applied to problems as wide ranging as clinical effectiveness, the reliability of equipment and the effects of training, in fact any countable events that can be tracked over time.

Correlational design examines the *relationships* between phenomenon rather than the differences between them and can be applied to two or more variables. Do note that correlational design does not demonstrate cause and effect. At one point, it was thought that sleeping with the light on caused myopia in children (Quinn *et al.* 1999); it was subsequently found (Zadnik *et al.* 2000) that myopic parents – frequently related to myopic children – tended to leave their children's night lights on!

There are various different contexts for this over-arching design. You may observe things which appear to be similar and may wish to see if the relationship is statistically significant; straightforward correlations may be most appropriate. If you are interested in the extent to which different factors affect an outcome, you will probably use multiple regression. Trying to make sense of multiple correlations, you could use factor analysis.

In experimental situations, you may wonder about the possibility of interactions between effects, which is where a factorial ANOVA comes into its own. Factorial ANOVA includes within-subjects, between-subjects and mixed-design variants.

A SUGGESTION FOR DATA ANALYSIS STRUCTURE

With research design decided upon, we may turn to data analysis. There are different ways of approaching problems. This is just one way of structuring your work.

Decide on what you wish to measure – have a rationale

Ideally, you will design data collation yourself, meeting your knowledge needs and making analysis easy. Often, however, you are given the data and left to analyse it. In either case, you need to decide on what to discriminate between, categorise or compare. As I hope will become clear, just shunting data into statistical software and hoping for significant 'results' is likely to mislead you and everybody else.

Examine the descriptive statistics

Data can be analysed numerically and graphically. Here, we are mainly interested in how SPSS allows you to examine the numbers.

Examining continuous data: between subjects

Just as SPSS requires a particular kind of data input for between-subjects design, using category or 'grouping variables', so the analysis of data is rather specific.

Open the 'Different' file we created in the previous chapter. From the menu at the top, select *Analyze/Compare Means/Means*. Highlight 'Score' and put it in the 'Dependent List' by pressing the relevant arrow; this is the 'dependent variable' (or target or criterion), that which is being measured as the study outcome. Then highlight Condition, Iron status or whatever is the relevant categorical variable to place it in the 'Independent List' (the independent variable, or predictor, is the variable manipulated to achieve the results). You may also view the medians by going into 'Options', following on with 'Continue'.

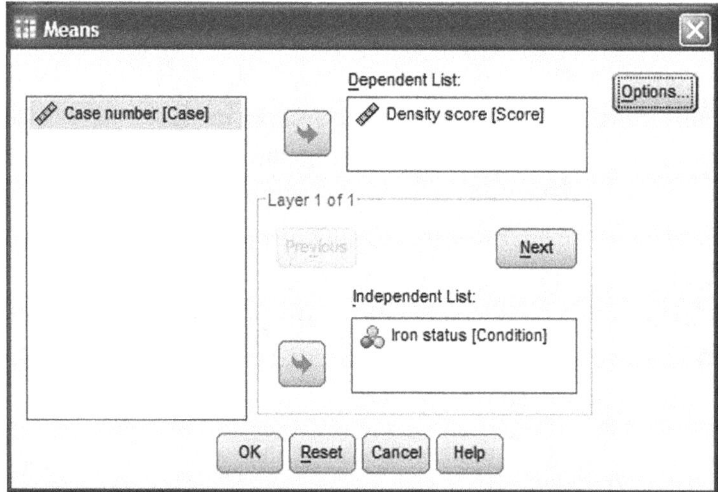

(Notice the symbols by the variables. The rule denotes that the measure chosen in the Dependent List is 'Scale'. The symbol beside the iron variable is for the 'Nominal' measure. The

'Next' button allows 'layering', the introduction of another variable, such as gender, for breaking up the data.)

Then press 'OK'.

Report

Density score

Iron status	Mean	N	Std. Deviation	Median
ferrous	44.00	5	10.840	45.00
non-ferrous	45.60	5	4.393	45.00
Total	44.80	10	7.843	45.00

The SPSS Viewer makes its first appearance. After a case summary (not shown) which allows us to check that we have captured the appropriate data, we see the two categories and also the combined sample, with read-outs for the mean, number of cases, Standard Deviation (*SD*) and the median. Additional statistics from 'options' could have included the range, variance and the sums of the two different sets of scores.

More comprehensive information is provided by *Analyze/Descriptive Statistics/Explore*.

Generally, you will report at least the means of the data sets. Large differences between the means often indicate significant differences.

Examining continuous data: within subjects

After opening the 'Same' file, select from the menu at the top *Analyze/Descriptive Statistics/Descriptives*, which offers a basic comparison between the two conditions for the same cases. Transfer the two conditions, A and B, to the Variable(s) box and then press 'OK'.

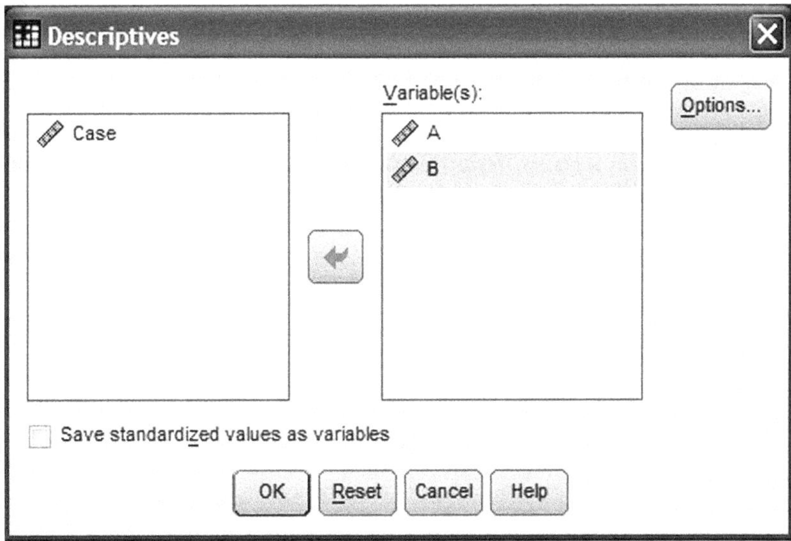

Here we see the different means for the two conditions. 'Options' could have provided us with additional statistics such as the variance and the sums of the two sets of scores.

Descriptive Statistics

	N	Minimum	Maximum	Mean	Std. Deviation
A	5	30.00	60.00	44.0000	10.83974
B	5	40.00	50.00	45.6000	4.39318
Valid N (listwise)	5				

Do note, however, that when dealing with non-parametric data, the median is preferred. Then you would use *Analyze/Descriptive Statistics/Frequencies.* In the Frequencies dialog box, transfer the 'A' and 'B' variables to the box on the right just as you did with Descriptives. Then select the 'Statistics' button on the right to select 'Median'. The output should provide the number of cases in each condition and the medians for each (here, 45 in both cases).

Examining ordinal and nominal data together

In this book, we consider ordinal data with relatively few categories (e.g. very light, light, medium, heavy, very heavy). Ordinal data with many categories could be treated as continuous data (and possibly tested for significance with parametric tests) or may be recoded into fewer categories.

Recoding

Returning to the 'Different' file, we can recode our current measurement data. We could use *Transform/Recode into Different Variables* (safer than overlaying your original data) or *Transform/ Visual Binning.* The Visual Binner, known in some SPSS editions as the Visual Bander, is available in the full and student versions of SPSS and we show a brief example of its use here.

Using the 'Different' file, select *Transform/Visual Binning.* Put Density score (Score) into 'Variables to Bin', then 'Continue'.

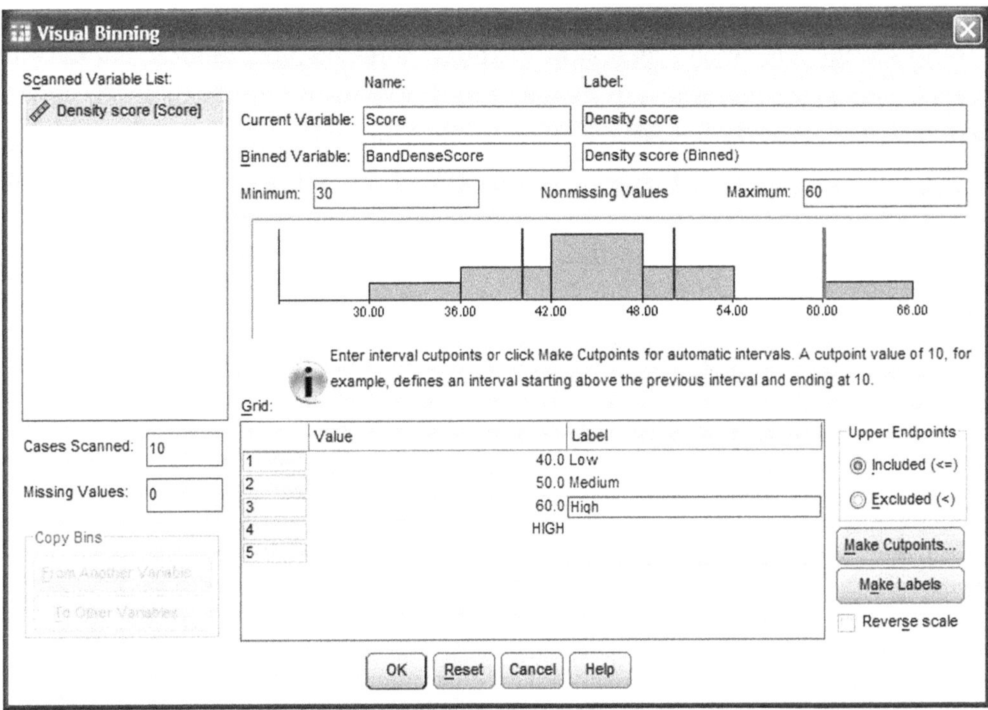

All that we have done here is to write a new variable name, BandDenseScore, next to 'Binned Variable', with a new label. In the grid, we have selected a score of 40 as the highest point for the band we have called 'Low', 50 for 'Medium' and 60 for 'High' (ignore the 'HIGH' value, a default). Then press 'OK'.

	Case	Score	Condition	BandDenseScore	Source
1	1	40	1	1	1
2	2	30	1	1	1
3	3	45	1	2	2
4	4	60	1	3	2
5	5	45	1	2	2
6	6	50	2	2	2
7	7	40	2	1	1
8	8	45	2	2	2
9	9	50	2	2	1
10	10	43	2	2	1
11					

Data View | Variable View

As you can see from Data View, a new variable has been created, BandDenseScore, with the number 1 representing the lowest score, 2 the medium score and 3 the highest, but the chosen banding names (here, Low, Medium and High) will appear in any output. Also, a new variable has been added, Source; in Data View, create 'Source' as the name and label, with Values of 1 for 'land' and 2 for 'sea' and input the numbers, into Data View as above (the condition labels can be viewed instead of the labels by selecting *View/Value Labels*).

Having recoded, we can examine the data, using *Analyze/Descriptive Statistics/Crosstabs* (cross-tabulation).

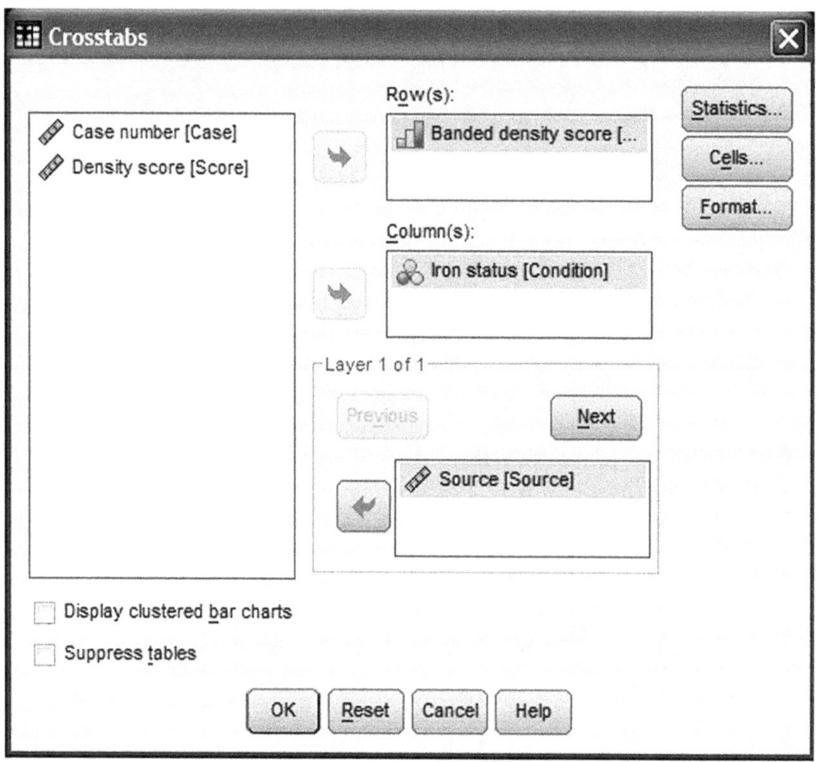

Variables with several values should be placed in rows, to avoid wide printouts. (Note the symbol by the banded variable denoting an ordinal measure.) The other item of interest goes in the columns box. 'Source' has been added to the cross-tabulation as a 'layer'; a 'Next' button is available for a further layer, but the more layers you have, the more difficult it is to analyse the 'Crosstabs' read-out.

Banded density score * Iron status * Source Crosstabulation

Count

Source			Iron status		Total
			ferrous	non-ferrous	
land	Banded density score	Low	2	1	3
		Medium	0	2	2
	Total		2	3	5
sea	Banded density score	Medium	2	2	4
		High	1	0	1
	Total		3	2	5

Even three variables make a relatively complicated cross-tabulation. It may be more informative not to use layers, but to show a series of pairings.

If you just want the count for the individual variables, use *Analyze/Descriptive Statistics/ Frequencies*. The banded test score, iron status and source may all be asked for at once, but the output will be in frequency tables of individual variables:

Banded density score

		Frequency	Percent	Valid Percent	Cumulative Percent
Valid	Low	3	30.0	30.0	30.0
	Medium	6	60.0	60.0	90.0
	High	1	10.0	10.0	100.0
	Total	10	100.0	100.0	

Similar boxes will appear for iron status (split into 'ferrous' and 'non-ferrous') and source ('land' and 'sea').

Nominal data and contingency tables

	Count	Agreement	Gender
1	1	1	1
2	2	1	1
3	3	1	2
4	4	2	2
5	5	2	2
6	6	3	1
7	7	3	1
8	8	3	2
9	9	3	2
10	10	3	2
11	11	3	2
12	12	3	2

Data View Variable View

In this survey example, Variable View has already been set up: its Agreement 'Values' are set with the following labels: 1 = Yes, 2 = No, 3 = Don't know. The Gender labels are 1 = Female and 2 = Male. The 'Measures' for both variables have been set to Nominal. (While it is possible to adjust these variables to Type 'string' to enter words such as 'Yes', we lose some functionality by doing so.) Remember to use a count variable; it helps us to keep track of what we are doing when files are manipulated.

We can use *Analyze/Descriptive Statistics/Frequencies* to read the frequency for each variable in a table. The Statistics option gives such statistics as the mean, median and mode. The data can be used to produce spreadsheet pie charts, which are easier to set up and adjust than SPSS charts.

However, to examine the relationship between these nominal variables, we need to create a contingency table. We use *Analyze/Descriptive Statistics/Crosstabs.*

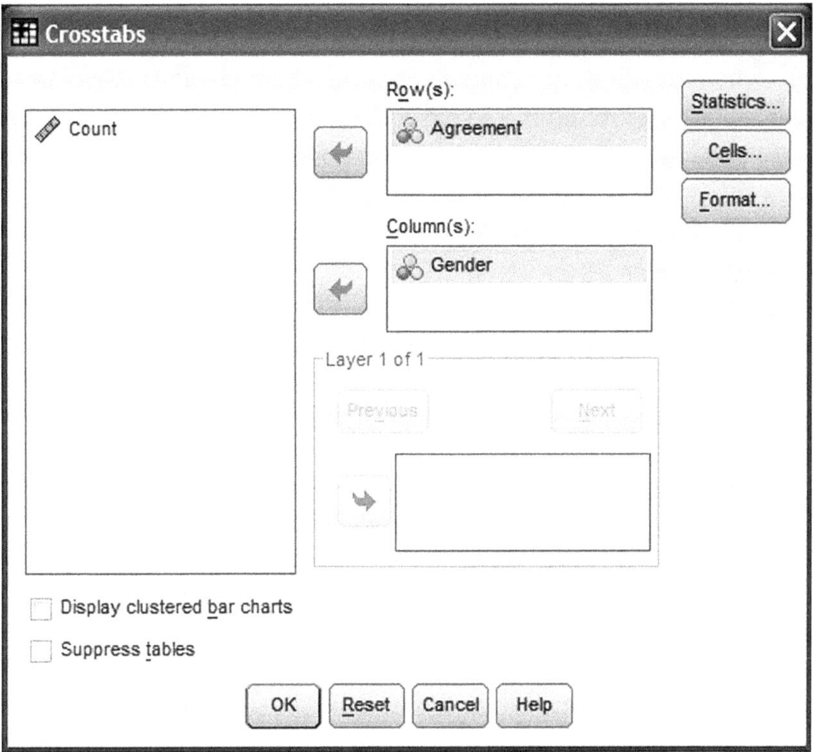

The variable with more options (3, as against 2 for gender) goes into 'Rows' to avoid too wide a read-out.

If we had more variables, the Layer box could be used to add another variable. When that is added, 'Next' can be used to add yet another. Although this may occasionally be useful, more variables in a contingency table tend towards difficult interpretation.

The Statistics box is used in the chapter on the frequency of observations.

The case processing summary (not shown here) is useful for checking for errors. '*N*' should equal the number of cases. The cross-tabulation will look like this:

Agreement * Gender Crosstabulation

Count

		Gender		
		Female	Male	Total
Agreement	Yes	2	1	3
	No	0	2	2
	Don't know	2	5	7
Total		4	8	12

Summary data and contingency tables

There will be times when we will wish to add summaries of data, frequencies instead of raw data. For example, we may wish to cross-tabulate subset data. For this purpose, we need to convert variables in Variable View to Type 'String' in order for them to be just names.

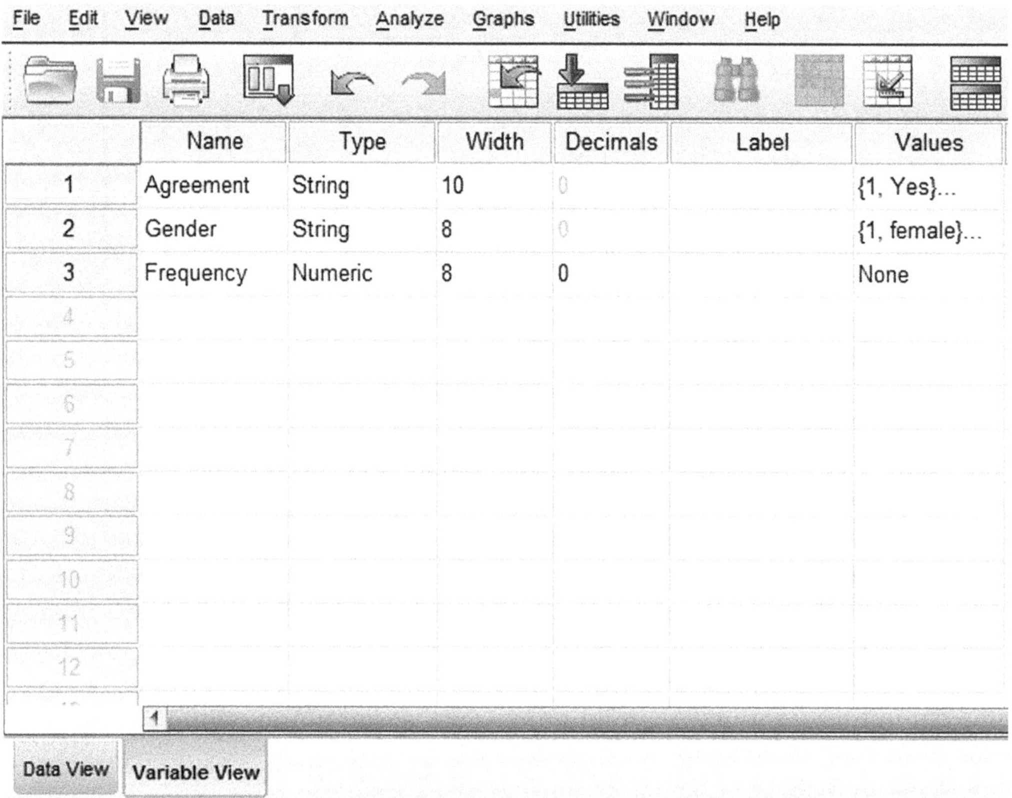

We give the Values labels as usual; the Agreement variable has been given a Width of 10 to contain 'don't know'. Most importantly, we have added a 'Frequency' variable with 'Decimals' set to zero.

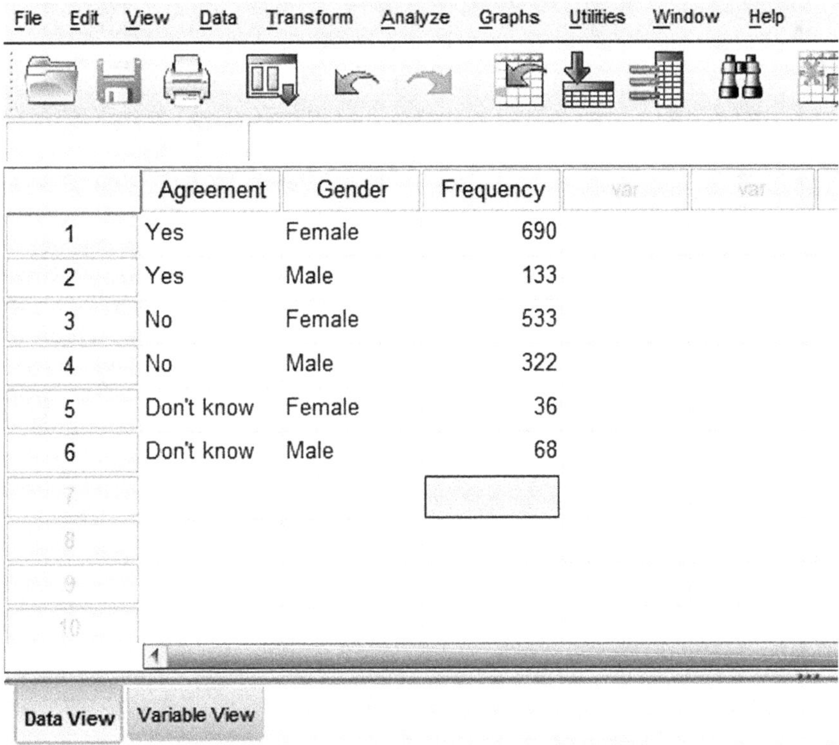

We then enter the possible summary data into Data View under 'Frequency'. Then use *Data/ Weight Cases*. Select 'Weight cases by' and transfer 'Frequency'. Press 'OK'. This allows Frequency to accept summary data.

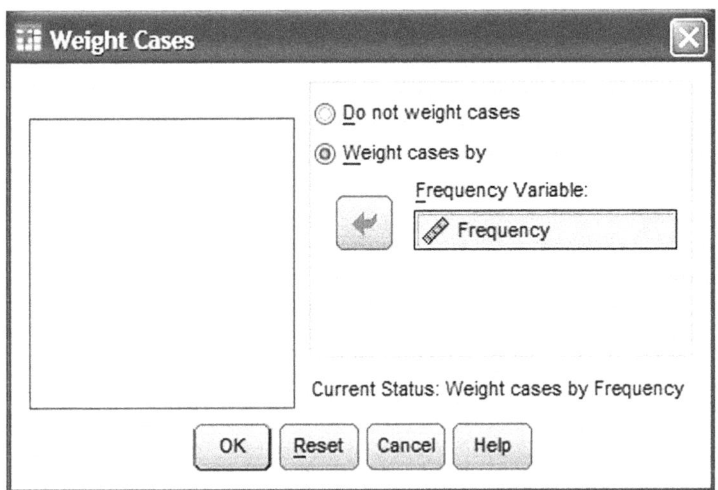

Some writers use the word 'Count', but I think 'Frequency' avoids confusion with the case numbers, which could produce some very peculiar results.

Then use *Analyze/Descriptive Statistics/Crosstabs.*

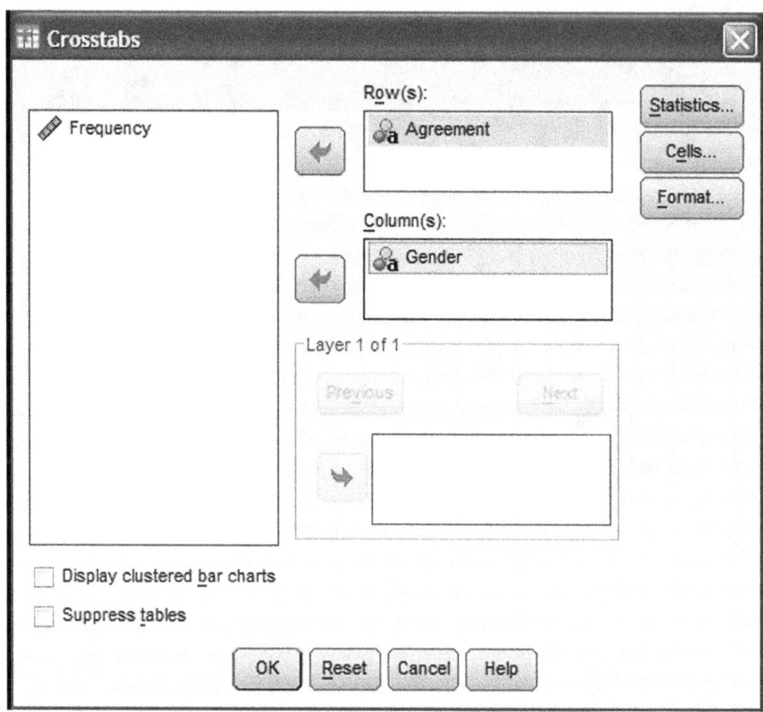

Agreement * Gender Crosstabulation

Count

		Gender		Total
		Female	Male	
Agreement	Don't know	36	68	104
	No	533	322	855
	Yes	690	133	823
Total		1259	523	1782

This table does not look much more informative than the original input. However, with more complicated subsets and when testing for the significance of qualitative data, this becomes very useful.

Examine your data in closer detail

As will be seen later, the data is not always as it seems. For continuous and ordinal data, you can find more detailed statistics using *Analyze/Descriptive Statistics/Explore.* Grouping variables can be placed in the 'Factor List', providing a breakdown of information into category groups. The 'plots' option may be selected in order to create box plots (it is also possible to use the SPSS 'Graphs' menu for this purpose). Box plots are particularly useful for detecting outliers.

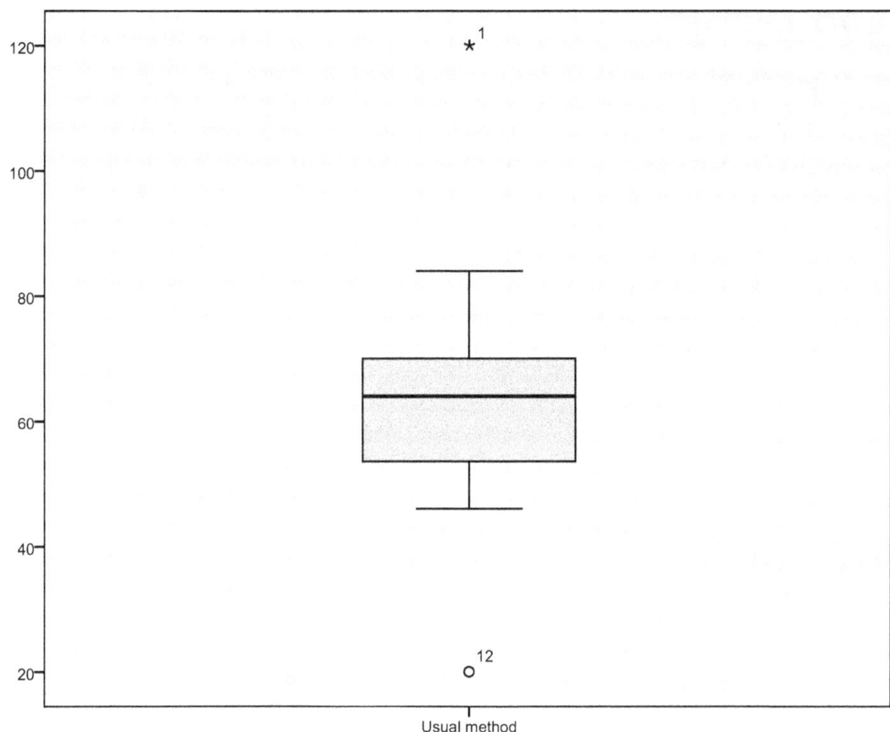

Two outliers are shown here. The circle represents a regular outlier. The asterisk or star represents an extreme outlier, one with a value three times the height of the box. The box itself represents 50% of the data, the bottom of the box representing the 25th percentile, or upper quartile, the top representing the 75th percentile (yep, the lower quartile). The whiskers, also known as inner fences, contain about 95% of the data. The central line is the median.

Decide which test to use

This will be discussed in detail in the rest of the book. However, one thing always worth doing is examining the distribution. To generate a distribution chart, use *Graphs/Chart Builder*, select a simple histogram and put the relevant data into the x axis. Then press the 'Element Properties' button and select 'Display normal curve'; press 'Apply'. Press 'OK' to see the output. As well as the data's distribution, there will be a comparison with the normal distribution.

To decide if parametric tests are applicable, however, it is recommended that you use *Analyze/ Descriptive Statistics/Explore*. Use 'Plots', selecting 'Normality plots with tests'. The Shapiro–Wilk test is for data sets of less than 50; use the Kolmogorov–Smirnov for larger numbers. If the test is significant, then the data set probably does *not* have a normal distribution. Descriptions of how to use these tests for different subjects design and same subjects design are given in the exercises on the Unpaired *t* test and Paired *t* test respectively.

Record and report

You should record decisions you make, including the omission of data. Spreadsheet charts are generally easier to modify than SPSS charts. Means (or medians, for non-parametric data) and relevant labels may be transferred to a spreadsheet such as Microsoft Excel for the creation of additional charts. So can cross-tabulations of frequencies. Remember to 'paste special' to a text format rather than into picture format.

When transferring between-subjects raw scores onto a spreadsheet, data conversion is needed to split up the data from the different groupings so that they can be lined up beside each other in columns on the spreadsheet. This conversion can be undertaken in an automated way using 'Select cases'.

SELECTING CASES

One method of examining data in a detailed way is by **selecting cases**. As an example we can examine iron status by viewing ferrous and non-ferrous separately. In our 'Different' file, non-ferrous was coded '2'. On the menu, select *Data/Select Cases*. Select the 'If condition is satisfied' option, then the 'If' button.

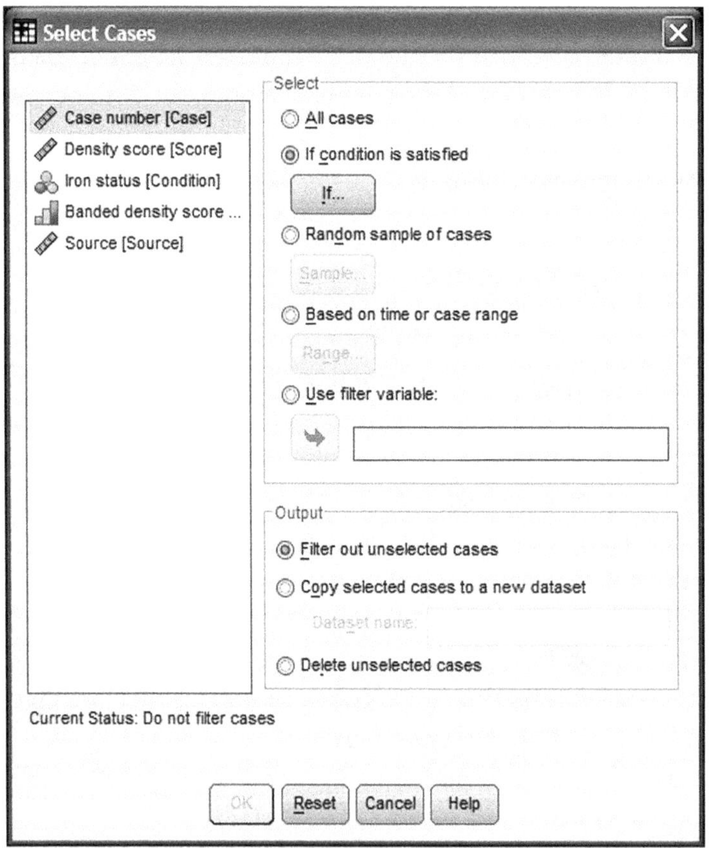

In the 'If' dialog, highlight 'Iron status' on the left, pressing the arrow to transfer it to the right. Then type or click the '=' button (note: the '~=' button means 'not equal to'), then the number. Then we have Condition = 2.

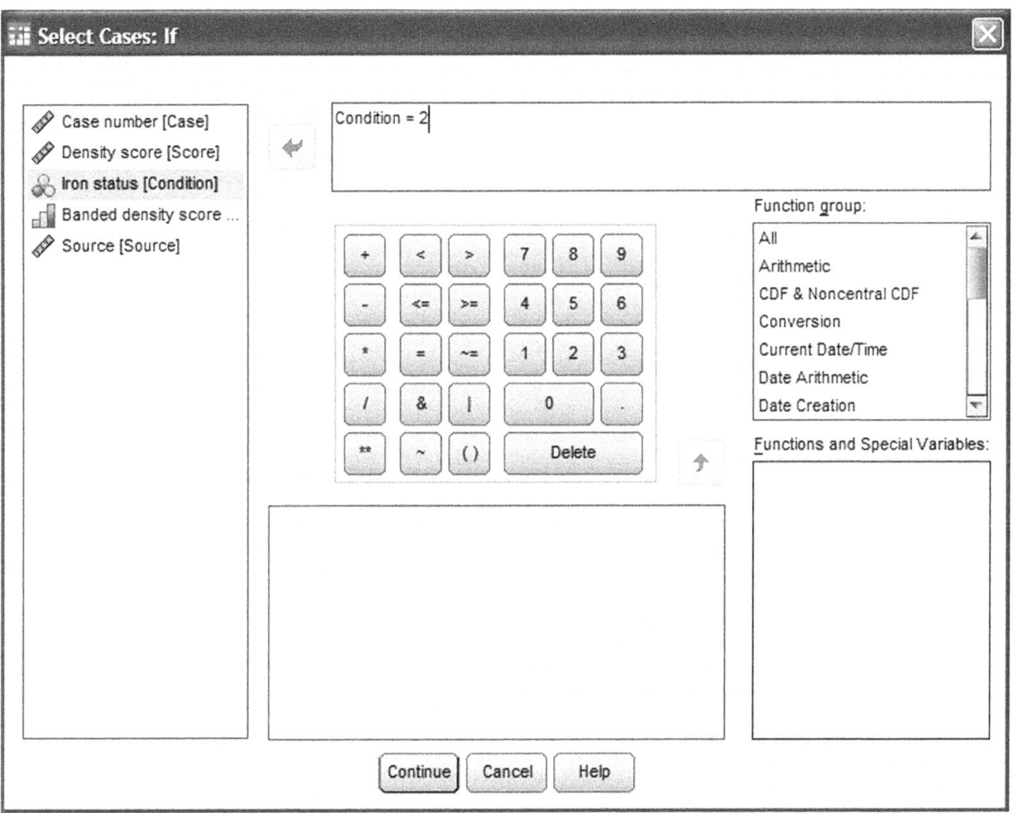

Pressing 'Continue' leads back to the 'Select Cases' dialog box; then press 'OK'. The status bar reminds us 'filter on' and diagonal lines on some of the far left gray tabs of Data View denote deselected cases. Any analysis of variables in the data set will only apply to the non-ferrous cases.

	Case	Score	Condition	BandDenseScore	Source	filter_$
1	1	40	1	1	1	
2	2	30	1	1	1	
3	3	45	1	2	2	
4	4	60	1	3	2	
5	5	45	1	2	2	
6	6	50	2	2	2	
7	7	40	2	1	1	
8	8	45	2	2	2	
9	9	50	2	2	1	
10	10	43	2	2	1	

Remember to check the status, currently 'Filter On', so that you know whether or not you are analysing the whole sample or a sub-sample.

To reverse this, go to *Data/Select Cases*; opt for 'All Cases' on the Select Cases dialog box and press OK.

OTHER DATA MANIPULATION TECHNIQUES

Another data handling technique in the Data sub-menu is **Split Files**, which allows you to examine data sets by breaking up the measure of interest according to one or more grouping variables. Remember to 'reset' to reverse the process.

Another technique is **Sort Cases**. This and other techniques are described in the SPSS Help file and other reference sources.

REPORTING DATA

This is discussed later in the book.

DISCUSSION POINT

It is important to examine data in a graphical format before getting carried away with the results of your statistical test. The data needs to be suitable for the test.

PART TWO

Using the statistical tests

CHAPTER 6

Experiments and quasi-experiments

THE ANALYSIS OF DIFFERENCES

It is presumed here that you have already considered research design. With the exception of factorial ANOVA, covered much later in this chapter, the focus here is on testing for significant *differences* between data sets.

UNRELATED AND RELATED DESIGN

In **unrelated design**, different participants/records are used in each condition. If we are testing for differences between the metabolisms of people in areas with hard water and soft water, then the cheapest and easiest method would be to run a quasi-experiment, testing people where they live. The participants in each area would of course be different individuals. In the case of people who are tested experimentally, offered either hard or soft water to drink, the consideration of order and other carry-over effects may also make you consider an unrelated design. There is of course an obvious problem, however: any test has to take into account a range of individual differences and is going to differ from a test applied to related designs.

Related design attempts to eliminate individual differences by either using the same subjects – the same person drinks both types of water at different times – or by the **pairing** (or **matching**) of different participants for particular characteristics, such as age, size and gender.

Here are some alternative terms you may come across:

Table 6.1

Unrelated design	**Related design**
Different subjects/participants	Same subjects/participants
Between subjects	Within subjects
Unpaired	Paired
Unmatched	Matched
	Repeated measures (repeated over time) Panel data (used in business statistics and econometrics; the same people over time)

TWO OR MORE CONDITIONS

We can cope with more than two conditions. These could be differing levels of water quality or in the case of medical treatments, a range of different therapies (T1, T2, T3).

DATA TYPE

This chapter deals with measurable data, where each observation can be compared numerically. For nominal (categorical) data, see the chapter on frequency observations.

RESEARCH DESIGN TERMINOLOGY

If we give our participants different drinks and measure the effects, we are running an **experiment** (even if not strictly controlled). We are manipulating **variables**, which are changeable (variable). We are actively manipulating an **independent variable**, the quality of the water. It could instead be the effect of different types of medical treatment, or a single treatment effect compared to a control. We observe the effect of manipulating the independent variable by looking at changes in the **dependent variable**, that which is being measured. The independent variable is varied according to the will of the experimenter, independent of real life perhaps, with the dependent variable being the data dependent on this variation. While these terms should strictly speaking be restricted to experimental work, they are widely used in other contexts.

Many 'real world' analyses of differences between data sets are **quasi-experimental**. We do not actively manipulate variables but use records or observations. Similarly, pairing/matching is performed by selecting from records rather than actually selecting experimental subjects. In a quasi-experimental version of our water studies, the effect of water quality would be called a **predictor** (rather than an independent variable) and the metabolism would be the **criterion** (rather than the dependent variable). The criteria for measurement could also be time of recovery from illness, the number of relapses, body weight, etc.

The terms predictor and criterion should be used in non-experimental research, but these are often interchangeable with independent and dependent variables in the literature. Both terms are used in this example (ignore the results, with imaginary figures and an unusable tiny data set).

Table 6.2

	Independent variable/predictor: Water type	
	Condition 1: Hard	**Condition 2: Soft**
Dependent variable/criterion: Metabolism (fictional)	400 300 450 600 450	500 400 450 500 430

And now, to the tests!

DIFFERENT SUBJECTS, TWO CONDITIONS

Parametric version: Unpaired *t* test (or 'independent *t* test')

We are examining the effects of fertilisers on agricultural soil function. Expensive fertiliser is used on some plots, cheap fertiliser on the others. The dependent variable is the biomass after fertiliser application for each plot expressed as a percentage of the mean.

DATA ENTRY

In Excel, the scores would generally be in two columns, one for cases 1 to 14 and the other for 15 to 26. In SPSS, *between-subjects data sets are input differently*, as in the following table. We use just one column, as each case must have its own row, but we also create a grouping variable (here, 1 for Expensive and 2 for Cheap).

Table 6.3

	Dependent variable: Biomass for each plot	**Independent variable: Fertiliser type**
Cases	**Percentage of the mean**	**Expensive vs. Cheap**
Plot 1	80	1
Plot 2	68	1
Plot 3	77	1
Plot 4	78	1
Plot 5	85	1
Plot 6	82	1
Plot 7	79	1
Plot 8	76	1
Plot 9	77	1
Plot 10	83	1
Plot 11	84	1
Plot 12	82	1
Plot 13	81	1
Plot 14	80	1
Plot 15	56	2
Plot 16	69	2
Plot 17	73	2
Plot 18	70	2
Plot 19	61	2
Plot 20	65	2
Plot 21	59	2
Plot 22	60	2
Plot 23	53	2
Plot 24	61	2
Plot 25	62	2
Plot 26	71	2

(Note that this study has different numbers of subjects in the different conditions; only 'same subject' studies must have the same numbers.)

Open SPSS and choose 'Type in data'. In Variable View in the SPSS Data Editor, each Name variable needs a name. On row 1, call it 'Case'; row 2 'Score'; row 3 'Fertiliser'. In each case, set

‘Decimals’ to zero. In the Label column, rename Case as ‘Plot Number’, Score as ‘Biomass Score’ and Fertiliser as ‘Fertiliser Type’. We want meaningful names for the fertiliser types, so go to the Fertiliser variable’s Values column and click the dotted area to the right of the cell. In the dialog box, add 1 to the *value* field in the dialog box and ‘expensive fertiliser’ in the *label* field, then press ‘Add’. Do the same with 2 and ‘cheap fertiliser’. These labels will appear in the output instead of the numbers. The Fertiliser row should be set to ‘Nominal’ in the Measure column (on this occasion, we are not interesting in ranking these categories). If you set all three Decimal settings to zero, you can get rid of annoying trailing zeroes in Data View.

In Data View, enter the scores and group number as in the table. As noted previously, you do not have to enter the case numbers manually. After entering in the data as above, use *Transform/ Compute Variable* and $CASENUM. (Case is your ‘target variable’ and ‘Plot Number’ should be in the label box. $CASENUM is the ‘numeric expression’.)

‘Save as’ to a ‘fertiliser’ file which you will use again later. It is good practice to save regularly during input in case of a program freeze.

ANALYSIS

If we want to use a parametric test, we should check for a normal distribution: *Analyze/Descriptive Statistics/Explore.* Use the ‘Plots’ button to select ‘Normality plots with tests’.

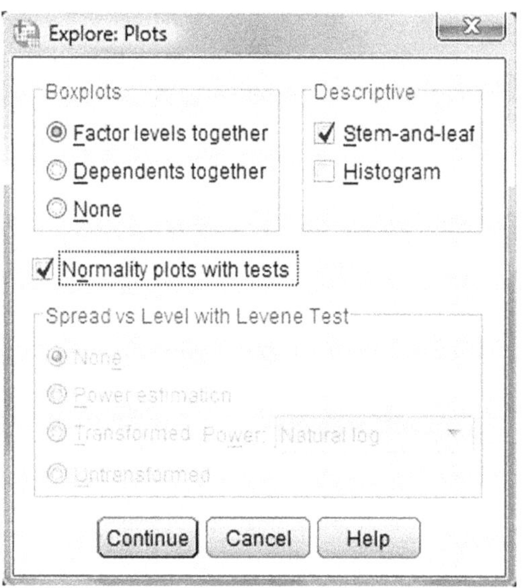

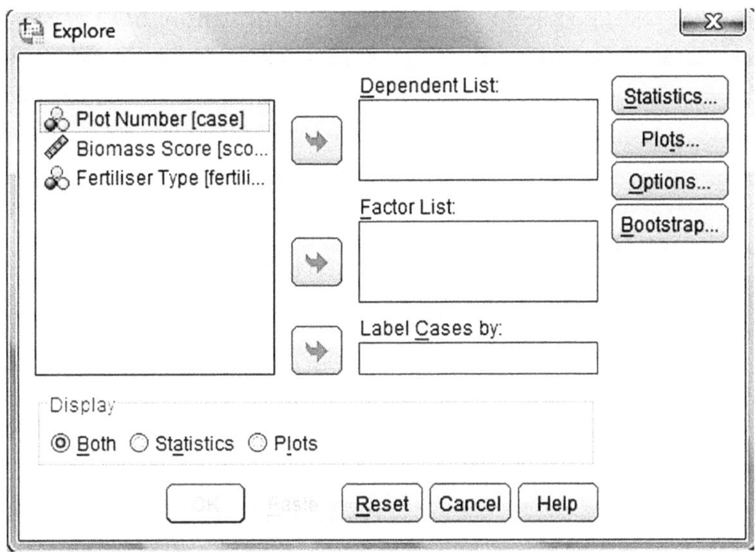

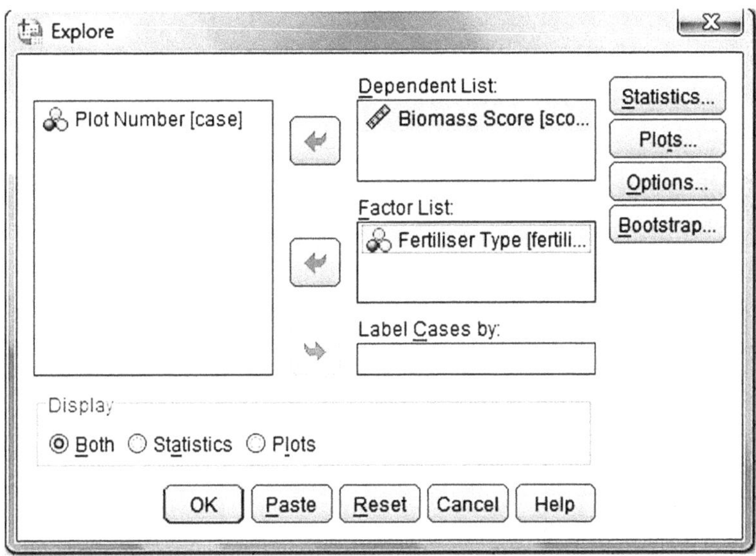

Transfer the score to the 'Dependent List' and the grouping variable (fertiliser type) to the 'Factor List'. Press 'OK'. The Shapiro–Wilk test result is for data sets of up to 50; read the Kolmogorov–Smirnov for 50 or more.

Tests of Normality

		Kolmogorov-Smirnov[a]			Shapiro-Wilk		
	Fertiliser Type	Statistic	df	Sig.	Statistic	df	Sig.
Biomass Score	expensive fertiliser	.142	14	.200*	.898	14	.104
	cheap fertiliser	.167	12	.200*	.952	12	.673

*. This is a lower bound of the true significance.

a. Lilliefors Significance Correction

Here, the Shapiro–Wilk test gives high *p* values, non-significant in both cases. The data is usable. (If the data is not normally distributed, consider using the Mann–Whitney test, which is non-parametric.)

Analyze/Compare Means/Independent–Samples t *Test.* The score goes into the upper right-hand box. When we transfer the grouping variable into its box, we see something strange:

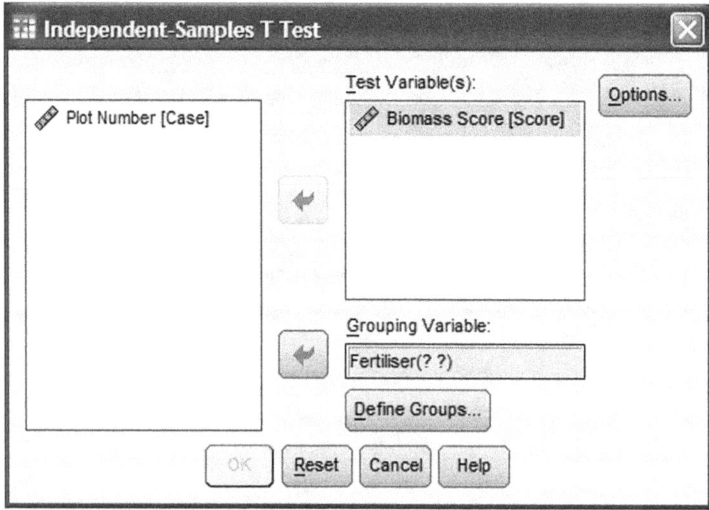

We need to press 'Define Groups' in order to provide SPSS with the values we have given to the groups, here 1 and 2.

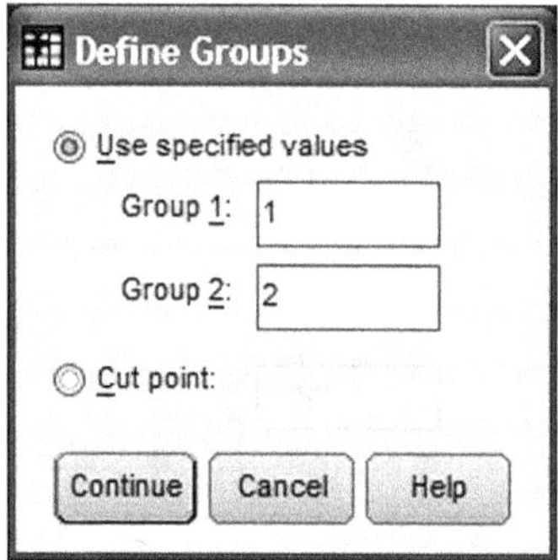

After typing in the two grouping variable values, press 'Continue'; the grouping variable box should now show 'Fertiliser(1 2)'. Then press 'OK' in the main dialog box in order to run the test.

If there are different numbers of cases in each group, as in this example, the data requires homogeneity of variance. The Levene test, integral to the read-out, examines this precondition. As with the tests of normality, the Levene test needs to be *non-significant* to show that the homogeneity assumption has been met.

If the Levene result is significant, *p* being equal to or smaller than .05, then we would either need to use the non-parametric equivalent test, the Mann–Whitney, or to provide equal numbers of cases for the two data sets. The second option is questionable, as the removal of data (in a small sample) may affect the outcome; if we added new data, we would need to be sure of its consistency.

The Levene result here gives a *p* value of .08, not significant, so we can continue using a parametric test with data of different sizes.

The Group Statistics read-out shows mean scores of 79.43 and 63.33 for the 'expensive fertiliser' and 'cheap fertiliser' conditions respectively. The *t* test shows a highly significant difference between the test scores, smaller than .001 two-tailed. According to this (fictional) data, the cheap fertiliser is considerable less effective than the expensive fertiliser. Please retain this file ('fertiliser') which will be extended later for the between-subjects ANOVA.

Non-parametric version: Mann–Whitney

One cohort of novice computer programmers is starting to use the Java programming language, another is to use Python. The same programming assignment has been given to both cohorts. The dependent variable consists of errors counted by the tutors.

DATA ENTRY

In Excel, we would use two columns of data. In SPSS data sets, each case must have its own row, so *input for between-subjects data sets is handled differently in SPSS*, as shown in the following table:

Table 6.4

	Dependent variable: Number of errors per student	**Independent variable: Programming language**
Cases	**Errors**	**Java vs. Python**
1	5	1
2	4	1
3	16	1
4	6	1
5	7	1
6	22	1
7	8	1
8	9	1
9	9	1
10	8	1
11	6	2
12	15	2
13	4	2
14	4	2
15	6	2
16	7	2
17	16	2
18	7	2
19	5	2
20	4	2

The two conditions are represented as grouping variables 1 and 2.

Open SPSS and choose 'Type in data'. In Variable View, type suitable titles in the Name column, e.g. 'Case' on row 1, 'Errors' on row 2 and 'Language' on row 3. For each variable, set 'Decimals' to zero. Type in more meaningful names under Label, e.g. Case becomes 'Student Number', Errors becomes 'Number of Errors' and Language becomes 'Programming Language'. For meaningful use of Programming Language, we should give names to the grouping variables. To do this, we need the cell where the Language row and Values column intersect, clicking the dotted area to the right of the cell. In the dialog box, add 1 to the *value* field in the dialog box and 'Java' in the *label* field, then pressing 'Add', doing the same with 2 and 'Python'. These labels will appear in the output instead of the numbers. The Language row also needs an alteration in the Measure column; 'Nominal' is required, as we do not intend to rank these categories. Set all three 'Decimals' to zero to get rid of trailing decimal points. Press 'OK'.

Then input data via Data View. As noted previously, you do not have to enter the case numbers manually. After entering in the data as above, use *Transform/Compute Variable* and $CASENUM. Then save the file (maybe 'programming').

ANALYSIS

You should first examine the descriptive data using *Analyze/Descriptive Statistics/Explore*, as in the previous example. As this is non-parametric data, the median is the statistic of immediate interest; unlike means, these are not sensitive to outliers. We see medians of 8 and 6.

To test for significant differences between the medians, we use the Mann–Whitney test. *Analyze/Nonparametric Tests/Independent Samples.* Use the 'Fields' tab at the top: put the measure (Number of Errors) into 'Test Fields' and the grouping variable (Programming Language) into 'Groups'. Then press 'Run'.

We see a large significance value (.158). There is no significant difference between the data sets and thus no significant difference between the use of Java and of Python in this situation. You can save this data set (e.g. 'programming'), as it will be extended when we get to the Kruskal–Wallis test.

DIFFERENT SUBJECTS, MORE THAN TWO CONDITIONS

Parametric version: Between-subjects one-way ANOVA

Although the expensive fertiliser is clearly more productive than the cheap one, we may decide that the cost is prohibitive. If we were to try a fertiliser in the middling price range, would this produce better results than the cheap fertiliser?

DATA ENTRY

Open the file about fertilisers.

In Variable View, find the Fertiliser Type row and go to the Values column, clicking the dotted area to the right of the cell. Add 3 to the value field in the dialog box and 'middle price' in the label field, then press 'add'. So 3 is replaced by 'middle price' in the output.

In Data View, add the following 16 numbers at the bottom of the Score/Biomass Score column: 70, 70, 73, 80, 81, 75, 75, 73, 81, 76, 75, 75, 73, 71, 72, 67.

Add the running numbers 27 to 42 in the Case/Person Number column and '3' in the remaining cells of the Fertiliser column. Save the file (remember to save regularly when inputting larger data sets).

ANALYSIS

As usual we examine the descriptive data. *You should always analyse your data before running an ANOVA.* The data needs to be checked to see that it is normally distributed and suitably measurable. If you have equal numbers for each group, you do not need to worry about the third assumption, homogeneity of variance, which will be discussed when we see the read-out from the Levene test.

Analyze/Descriptive Statistics/Explore. Use the 'Plots' button to select 'Normality plots with tests'. Place the measure in the 'Dependent List' and the grouping variable into the 'Factor List'. Press 'OK'. With this data set, the Shapiro–Wilk test shows a non-significant result, so normality seems likely. (Read the Kolmogorov–Smirnov result if there are 50 or more cases.) If normality could not be assumed, we should use a non-parametric test.

Before moving away from the *Explore* read-out, we may extract the means, 79.43, 63.33 and 74.19. However, a quicker way of getting basic data with a clear output is to use *Analyze/Compare Means/Means.*

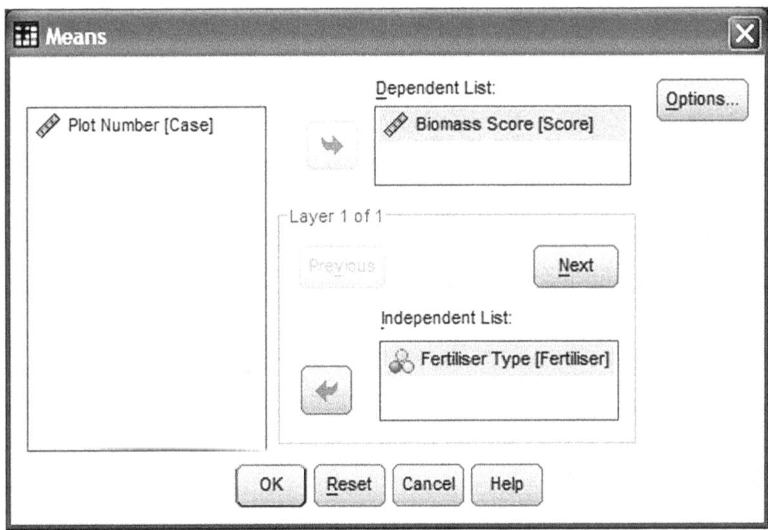

While the most expensive fertiliser produces significantly better results than the cheap one, it appears that the middle priced fertiliser is also effective. However, we do not yet know if the middle range fertiliser produces significantly better results than the cheap one; also, we do not know if the more expensive fertiliser remains significantly more productive when compared to the middle range product.

To test for significance, use *Analyze/General Linear Model/Univariate*. (*Analyze/Compare Means/One-Way ANOVA* is also usable but does not provide the Partial Eta Squared effect size statistic.)

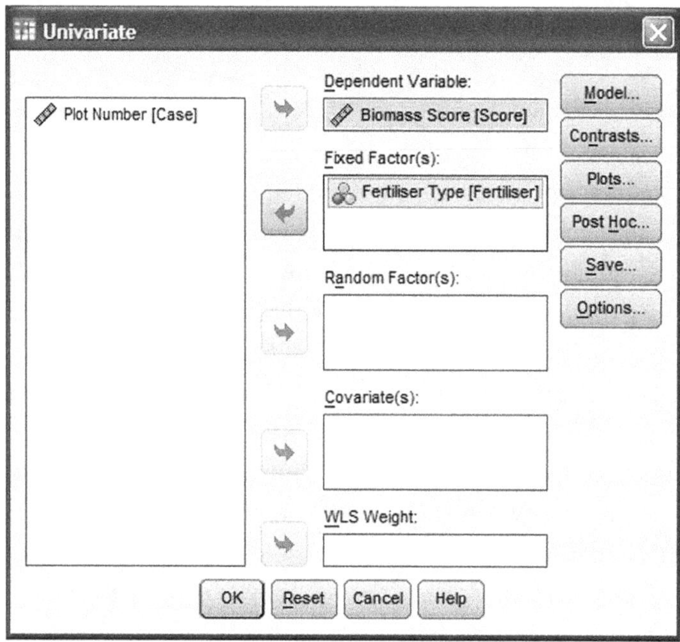

The Covariate box is for additional variables which may influence the interactions we are interested in. The analysis of covariance (ANCOVA) is in this researcher's opinion fraught with hazards, particularly related to the various assumptions which must be met. My misgivings are discussed in more detail at the end of the book. For the moment, I would just suggest ignoring this box. Similarly, the Random Factor(s) box is also an advanced procedure which I think should be avoided.

Press the 'Post Hoc' button. Move the relevant grouping category (Fertiliser) into the right-hand box and select 'Tukey', a test which examines the relationship between individual pairings. Press 'Continue'.

The 'Options' button allows us to select the Partial Eta Squared effect size statistic, which is useful if the main effect is significant. Also, we can adjust the significance level from its default of .05 if we so wish. If we have *uneven numbers* in our data subsets, we will want 'Homogeneity tests': the Levene Statistic would need to be non-significant.

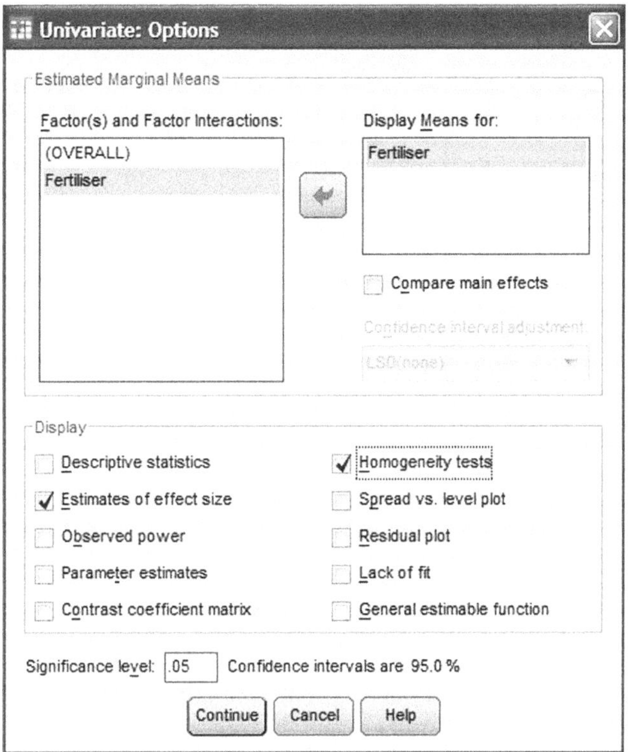

If the Levene test is significant, with a p value of .05 or less, then we would either turn to the non-parametric Kruskal–Wallis test or create data sets with the same number of cases.

Here, however, the Levene test is not significant (.089) so homogeneity of variance may be assumed and we can continue reading the ANOVA results.

Analysis of variance calculates how much of the variance derives from independent variables and how much is due to error (error variance). The calculation, the variance divided by the error, is the F ratio, referred to in the output as 'F'. The more the variable's effect outweighs the error, the bigger the F ratio and the more likely a significant result. The null hypothesis is that the means of the data groups are all equal.

When reading the 'Tests of Between-Subjects Effects' output table, ignore the 'Corrected Model' and 'Intercept' rows. Our interest is in 'Fertiliser', the main effect, which has an F ratio of 36.863, Sig. = .000, Partial Eta Squared .654. The overall differences between the conditions are highly significant, $p < .0005$. Partial Eta Squared, the estimated effect size, is .654, a medium-sized effect.

EFFECT SIZE AND THE ANALYSIS OF DIFFERENCES

One rule of thumb is that an effect size of 0.2 to 0.5 is small, 0.5 to 0.8 is medium and greater than 0.8 is large.

The 'Error' calculation you will see in the table represents within-group variance.

The Multiple Comparisons output table shows the 'post hoc' differences between each pair of variables, using the Tukey test.

Multiple Comparisons

Biomass Score
Tukey HSD

(I) Fertiliser Type	(J) Fertiliser Type	Mean Difference (I-J)	Std. Error	Sig.	95% Confidence Interval	
					Lower Bound	Upper Bound
expensive fertiliser	cheap fertiliser	16.10*	1.901	.000	11.46	20.73
	middle price	5.24*	1.768	.014	.93	9.55
cheap fertiliser	expensive fertiliser	-16.10*	1.901	.000	-20.73	-11.46
	middle price	-10.85*	1.845	.000	-15.35	-6.36
middle price	expensive fertiliser	-5.24*	1.768	.014	-9.55	-.93
	cheap fertiliser	10.85*	1.845	.000	6.36	15.35

Based on observed means.
The error term is Mean Square(Error) = 23.347.
* The mean difference is significant at the .05 level.

Each data row shows the data from the viewpoint of one of the conditions. The Mean Difference column shows the means for each condition subtracted from each other. The asterisks next to the differences represent significance; if the 'Options' significance setting had been adjusted to .01, two of them would have disappeared, as can be seen in the significance column. The differences between the expensive fertiliser and the cheap fertiliser, and between the middle range and cheap fertilisers are significant at $p < .0005$, whereas the difference between the expensive and middle range fertilisers is significant at $p < .02$. The confidence intervals show that 95% of the time, we can be sure that the Mean Difference will be within the upper and lower bounds; this would have been 99% if we had set 'Options' to .01.

Biomass Score

Tukey HSD [a,b,c]

Fertiliser Type	N	Subset		
		1	2	3
cheap fertiliser	12	63.33		
middle price	16		74.19	
expensive fertiliser	14			79.43
Sig.		1.000	1.000	1.000

Means for groups in homogeneous subsets are displayed.
Based on observed means.
The error term is Mean Square(Error) = 23.347.

a. Uses Harmonic Mean Sample Size = 13.808.

b. The group sizes are unequal. The harmonic mean of the group sizes is used. Type I error levels are not guaranteed.

c. Alpha = 0.05.

The Homogeneous Subsets chart shows which groups are significantly different from each other. Here, the means from each condition are all in different columns. If a column contained more than one statistic, the conditions within the column would not be significantly different from each other. This table would be more useful if we were examining a larger number of variables.

It looks like the middle range fertiliser is a sensible compromise between the two other fertilisers. At the same time, depending upon the value of the produce, using the most expensive fertiliser may still prove to be a valid option.

Non-parametric version: Kruskal–Wallis

Open the file with data on programming languages, previously used with the Mann–Whitney. We now have data on computing errors following the use of yet another programming language, this time Visual Basic.

This adds a third condition to our between-subjects design. The Kruskal–Wallis test is used as an extension of the Mann–Whitney.

DATA ENTRY

In Variable View, find the Programming Language row and in the Values column, click the dotted area to the right of the cell. Add '3' to the 'value' field in the dialog box and 'Visual Basic' in the 'label' field.

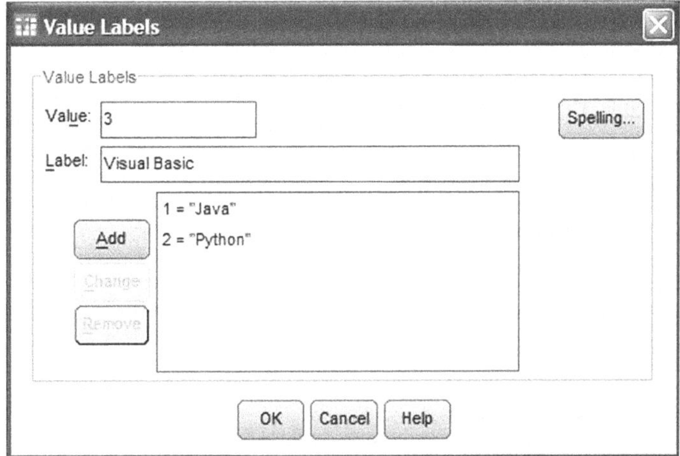

Then press 'Add'. The output will read 'Visual Basic' rather than the less than comprehensible '3'. Press 'OK'.

Then in Data View, add the following data to the Errors column: 8, 4, 3, 12, 4, 4, 9, 8, 32, 6. Add the running numbers 21 to 30 in the Case/Student Number column and the number 3 in the adjacent Programming Language column.

ANALYSIS

You can use *Analyze/Descriptive Statistics/Explore* for a large range of statistics including the medians, which are particularly of interest in non-parametrics. However, a faster view of the more basic statistics is achieved with *Analyze/Compare Means/Means* which is also a lot better for copying data, but you do need to press the 'Options' button to add the medians to the read-out.

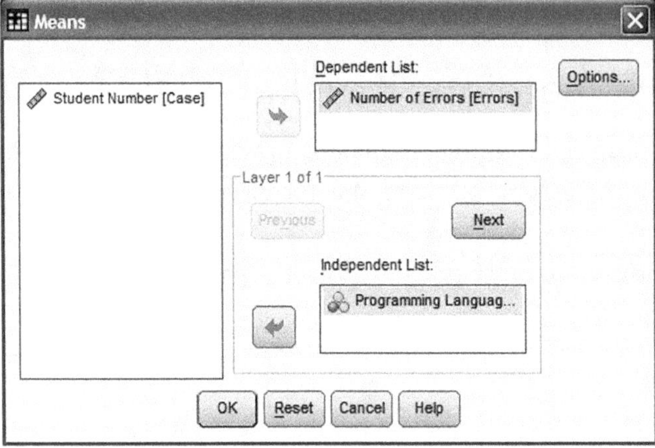

This provides a clear output of the basic statistics for each programming language, the medians being Java 8, Python 6 and Visual Basic 7.

To test for significant differences, use *Analyze/Nonparametric Tests/Independent Samples.* Use the 'Fields' tab at the top. Transfer the measure (number of errors) to the Test Fields box on the right and the grouping variable (programming language) into the 'Groups' slot.

After pressing 'Run', you will find that the output refers to the Kruskal–Wallis test. A non-significant result, p value = .409 shows that is no overall significant difference between the programming languages.

Testing individual pairings when there is no overall effect is possible, but be warned about seeking tenuous results: each individual test multiplies the likelihood of chance results. You could use the Mann–Whitney test for this. If you run *Analyze/Nonparametric Tests/Legacy Dialogs/Two Independent Samples*, you can compare the different subsets.

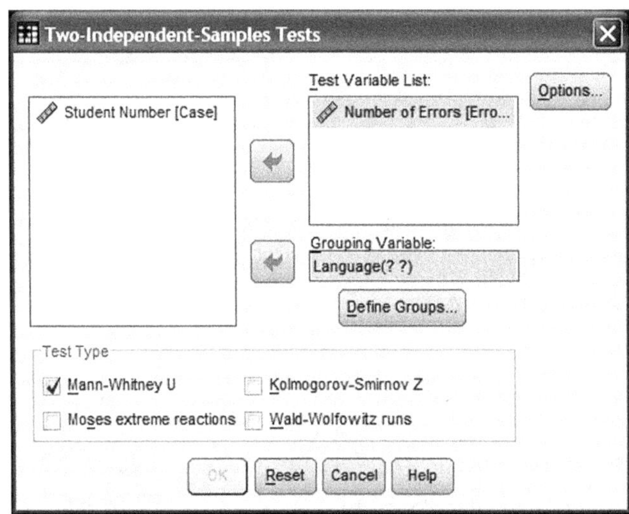

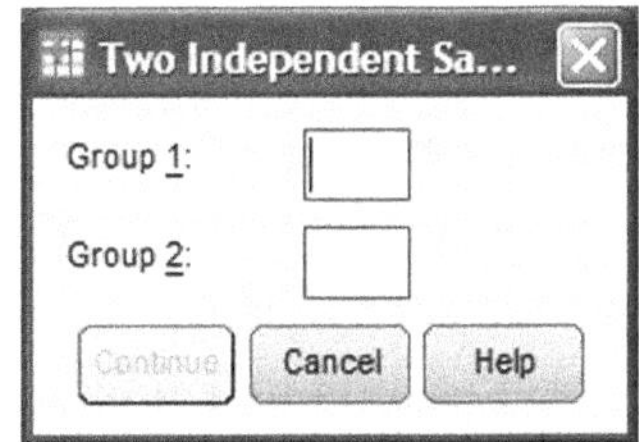

When you press the 'Define Groups' button, enter the relevant values, e.g. '1' and '3' for 'Java' and 'Visual Basic', and then press 'Continue', then 'OK'.

However, an increase in the number of potential false positives means that we should multiply our significance levels. The Bonferroni method requires multiplying the number of potential tests by the number of pairings. If, in a hypothetical case, we have three subsets with the significance level of one particular pairing being .021, then we have 3 × .021 = .063, non-significant. Some statisticians consider Bonferroni unnecessarily harsh, so I suggest multiplying by the number of pairings minus .5. So we multiply the significance values by 2.5: this would still give a non-significant result at $p < .05$ (2.5 × .021 = .0525).

SAME SUBJECTS, TWO CONDITIONS

Parametric version: Paired *t* test (or related *t* test)

Variation in the amount of water in wetlands can affect plant life (Ellery Mayence *et al.* 2010). Here we examine the biomass of a particular plant within a wetland region, each area of the region being studied twice, at two different levels of wetness. The biomass is expressed as a percentage of the mean.

Table 6.5 Predictor: Hydrologic regimes

		Condition 1: Inundated	**Condition 2: Saturated**
Criterion: Biomass (expressed as per cent)	Area 1	52	60
	Area 2	53	34
	Area 3	47	38
	Area 4	40	52
	Area 5	48	54
	Area 6	45	55
	Area 7	52	36
	Area 8	47	48
	Area 9	51	44
	Area 10	38	56

DATA ENTRY

Open SPSS and choose 'Type in data'. In Variable View, for each Name, type 'Area' as the first variable; 'Inundated' as the second variable; and then 'Saturated'. The Label for the first variable would be something like 'Area Number', the second becomes 'Inundated state' and the third, 'Saturated state'. All three Decimal settings should be adjusted to zero to get rid of trailing zeroes. With same-subjects (related) samples, we do not have grouping variables and so do not need 'Values' for transforming numbers.

Enter the figures in Data View. As noted previously, you do not have to enter the case numbers manually. After entering in the data as above, use *Transform/Compute Variable* and $CASENUM. Save the file as something like 'wetness'; the file will be extended a little later.

ANALYSIS

Check for normal distribution for both data sets, using *Analyze/Descriptive Statistics/Explore*. The 'Plots' button allows us to select 'Normality plots with tests'.

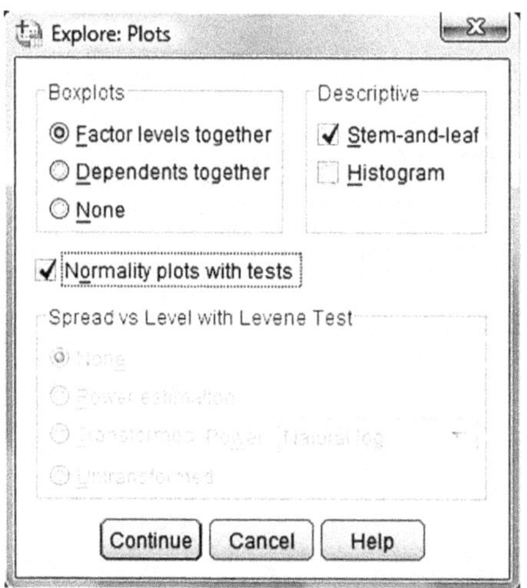

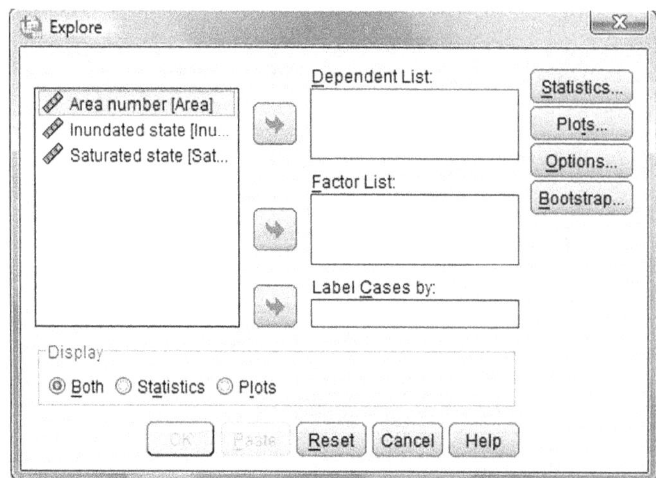

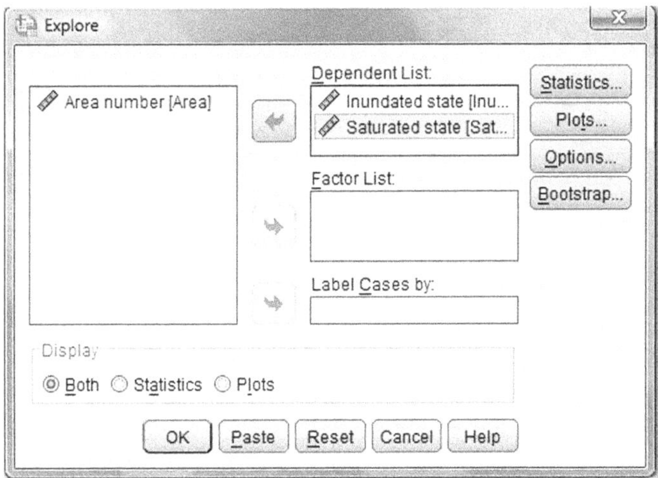

Put both 'Inundated' and 'Saturated' in the 'Dependent List'. Read the Shapiro–Wilk results for data sets of less than 50; for 50 or more, use Kolmogorov–Smirnov.

Tests of Normality

	Kolmogorov-Smirnov[a]			Shapiro-Wilk		
	Statistic	df	Sig.	Statistic	df	Sig.
Inundated state	.177	10	.200*	.901	10	.225
Saturated state	.180	10	.200*	.921	10	.365

*. This is a lower bound of the true significance.

a. Lilliefors Significance Correction

Here, the Shapiro–Wilk test shows *p* values of .225 and .365, both non-significant, so normality may be assumed. If the data is not normally distributed, you should use the non-parametric Wilcoxon test.

The Explore procedure indicates means of 47.3 and 47.7, a difference of 0.4, but is this significant? We test with *Analyze/Compare Means/Paired-Samples* t *Test*. Transfer 'Inundated state' and 'Saturated state' to the Paired Variables window on the right using the arrow. Press 'OK'.

The large *p* value (.922 two-tailed) indicates a non-significant difference. The difference in wetness between the inundated and saturated states appears not to affect the plant's biomass in a significant way.

Non-parametric version: Wilcoxon

Spectroscopy methods A and B are tested for their functionality. Various compounds are each analysed by both methods. The measure (or criterion) is a five point usefulness rating, higher scores being positive. If the rating scale had been calibrated for reliability, we may have considered a parametric test, but it has not, so a non-parametric test is more suitable. We adopt a .05 level of significance as we are using a small sample. Without theoretical reasons for one method being better than another, we choose the more rigorous two-tailed hypothesis.

Table 6.6

		Independent variable: Spectroscopy methods	
		Method A	**Method B**
Dependent variable: Usefulness	Compound 1	4	5
	Compound 2	3	3
	Compound 3	2	4
	Compound 4	4	5
	Compound 5	3	5
	Compound 6	4	2
	Compound 7	3	3
	Compound 8	5	4
	Compound 9	3	5
	Compound 10	4	5
	Compound 11	3	5
	Compound 12	2	4
	Compound 13	2	5

DATA ENTRY

Open SPSS and choose 'Type in data'. In Variable View, type 'Compound' in the first Name cell, type 'A' in row 2 and 'B' in row 3. Under Label, type in 'Compound number' (or 'Case number' if preferred), 'A Method' and 'B Method' respectively. To get rid of trailing decimal points, it is recommended that you set all three Decimal settings to zero. With same-subjects (related) samples, we do not have grouping variables and so we do not need 'Values' for transforming numbers.

Then in Data View, enter the figures as given in the table above.

As noted previously, you do not have to enter the case numbers manually. After entering in the data as above, use *Transform/Compute Variable* and $CASENUM.

Save the file, e.g. as 'spectroscopy'.

ANALYSIS

For non-parametric data, we prefer the median to the mean as the measure of central tendency. Use *Analyze/Descriptive Statistics/Frequencies*.

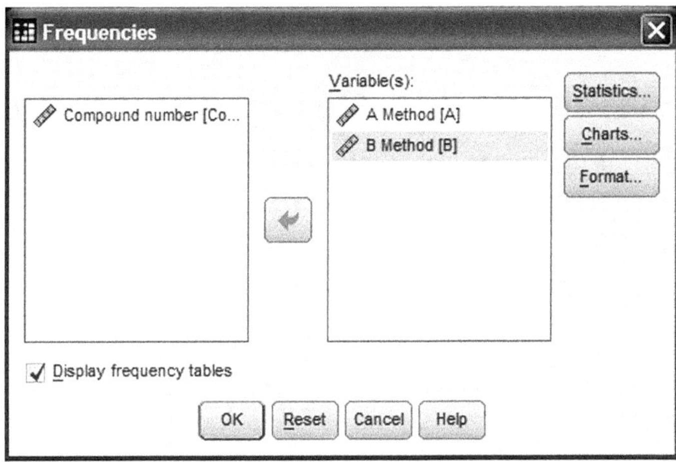

Use the 'Statistics' button to select the median (other statistics may also be chosen). The 'Charts' button provides graphical representation.

There is a considerable difference between the medians, 3 for 'A Method' and 5 for 'B Method'. The bar chart option illustrates these differences well. (If you opt for the histogram with a superimposed normal curve, you can see that the data is not normally distributed and is therefore unsuitable for a parametric test.)

To test if the difference between the variables is significant, we use the Wilcoxon test. One way is to use *Analyze/Nonparametric Tests/Related Samples*, using the 'Fields' tab at the top and transferring the measures (A Method, B Method) to the dialog box on the right. Press 'Run'.

The result is .036, so the null hypothesis can be rejected at a significance level of $p < .05$. If you select *Analyze/Nonparametric Tests/Legacy Dialogs/Two Related Samples* (the dialog box is shown below), you will see that the .036 represents a two-tailed result. When we have reason to expect a one-tailed test of significance, the critical value can be halved, but in this case (half of 0.05 is 0.25), it would not be low enough to declare the next usually quoted figure, $p < .02$.

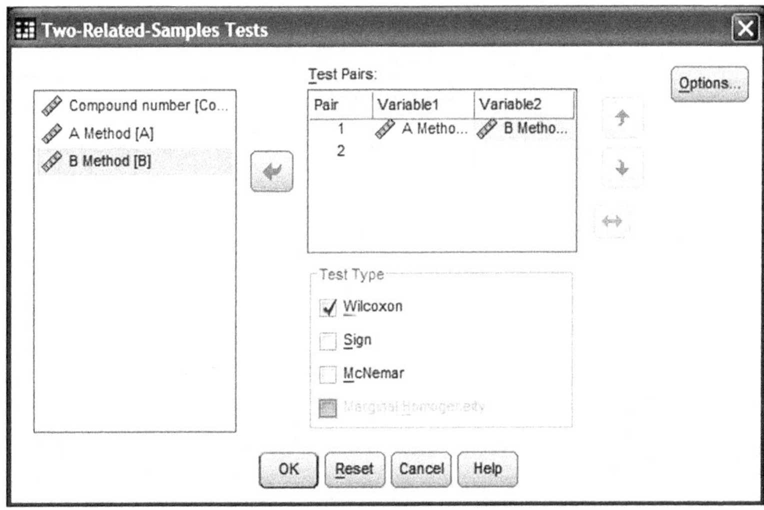

SAME SUBJECTS, MORE THAN TWO CONDITIONS

Parametric version: Within-subjects one-way ANOVA

The within-subjects analysis of variance, also referred to as a repeated-measures ANOVA, is used for more than two conditions. This test requires the SPSS Advanced Module. The alternative test is the Friedman, shown later.

* **Predictor:** Hydrologic regimes.
* **Condition** 1: Inundated **Condition** 2: Saturated **Condition** 3: Moist.

We are working on an extended version of our 'wetness' file. Our plant's biomass is now being compared over three conditions.

DATA ENTRY

Re-opening the wetness file, type 'Moist' in Variable View in the next row, with the label 'Moist state'. Set the Decimal column to zero. In Data View, enter the following 10 numbers alongside the other two data columns: 62, 56, 40, 37, 62, 56, 68, 55, 68, 60.

ANALYSIS

First examine the descriptive data. *You should always carry out EDA (exploratory data analysis) before running an ANOVA.* We need to check that the assumptions of normal distribution have been met and that the data is suitably measurable.

One option is to use *Analyze/Descriptive Statistics/Descriptives*, but more information is provided by *Analyze/Descriptive Statistics/Explore*. Transfer the three conditions to the Dependent Variables box and press the 'Plots' button for 'Normality plots with tests', then press 'OK'.

The Shapiro–Wilk test, for less than 50 cases, is not significant (Kolmogorov–Smirnov is for larger samples). So, there is no indication of abnormality in the new data. A parametric test is suitable. However, the Box plot for the 'Moist state' condition indicates two outliers among the new cases. In real life, you would need to check that cases 3 and 4 were not input errors.

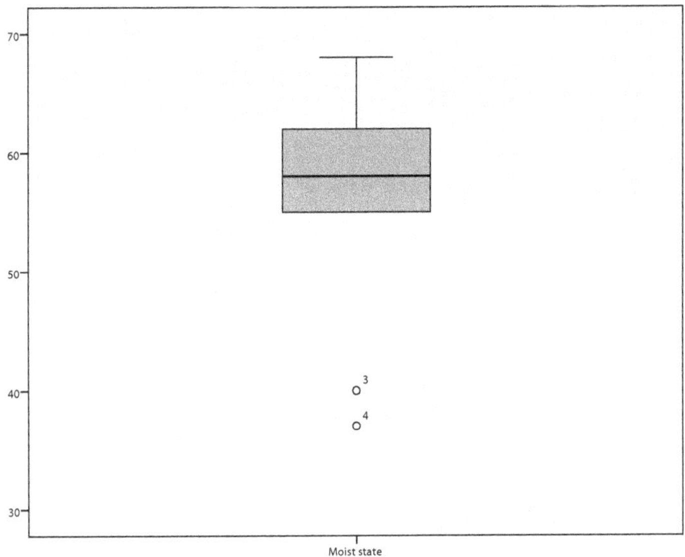

(In a box and whisker plot, the box represents 50% of the data. The thick line in the middle is the median. On either side of the median are the upper and lower quartiles, each representing 25% of the data. Most of the data is usually found within whiskers above and below the box. In this data set, there is no low score whisker, but we do see two outliers, '3' and '4'.)

As we have parametric data, we can use ANOVA. We choose *Analyze/General Linear Model/ Repeated Measures* (select 'General Linear *Model*', singular, not the 'General Linear *Models*' menu option). In the Repeated Measures Define Factor(s) dialog box, replace 'factor1' with an apt factor name (here, 'wetness'). All names in this dialog box must be eight or fewer characters, starting with a lower case letter. Then put the number 3 into the 'Number of Levels'.

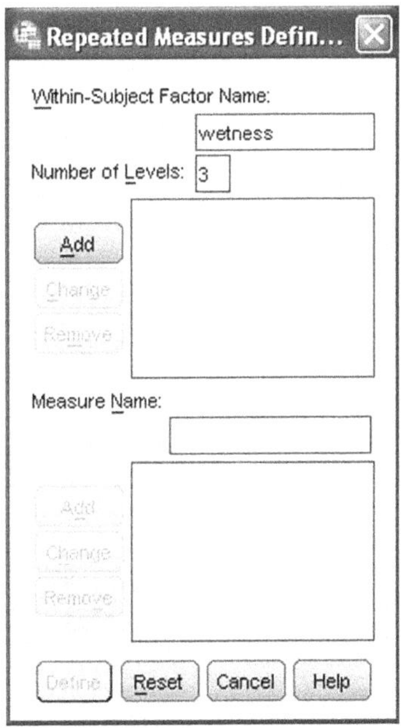

Then press 'Add' to get this:

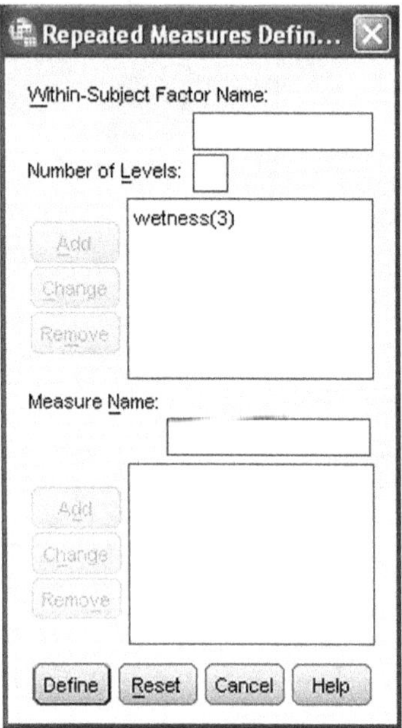

Type a dependent variable name in 'Measure Name':

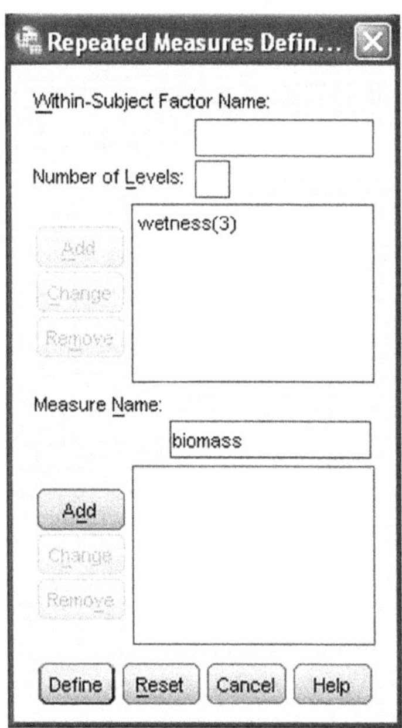

After pressing 'Add', the next image should appear. (People frequently have difficulty getting repeated-measures ANOVA to work, hence the detailed coverage here.)

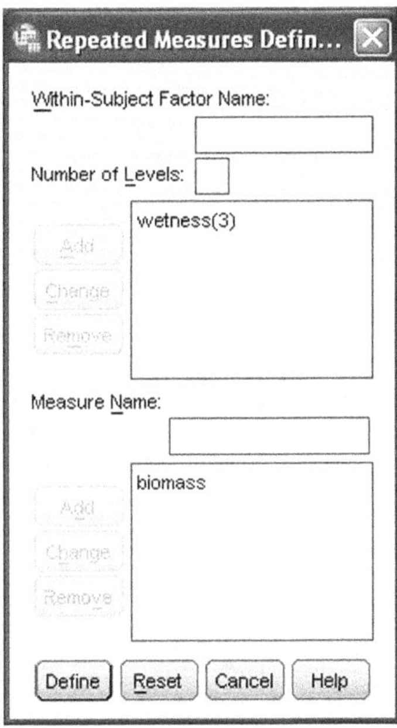

Then click 'Define' to go to the Repeated Measures dialog box. The variables Inundated, Saturated and Moist are transferred to the right, replacing the default question marks shown next:

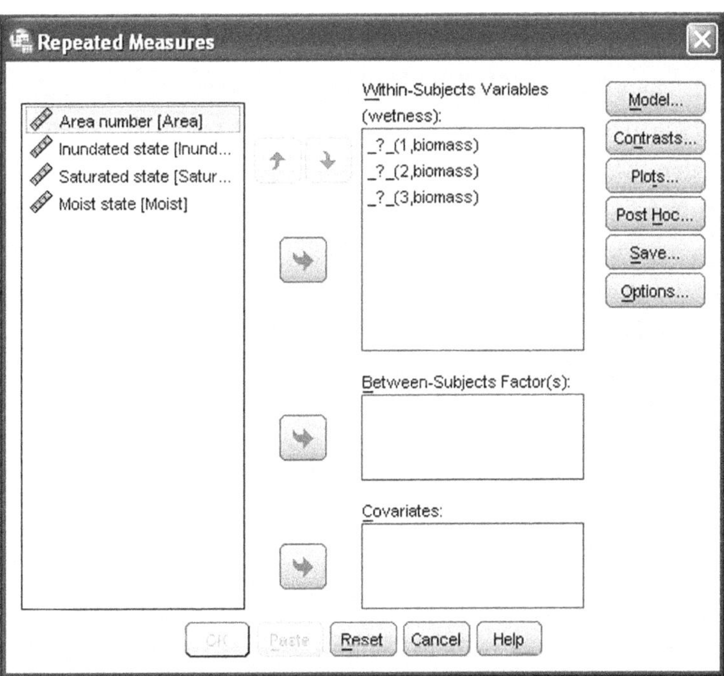

(ANOVA can become more complicated, especially when analysing more than one factor, so try getting into the habit of transferring one by one to avoid errors.) The finished box should look like this:

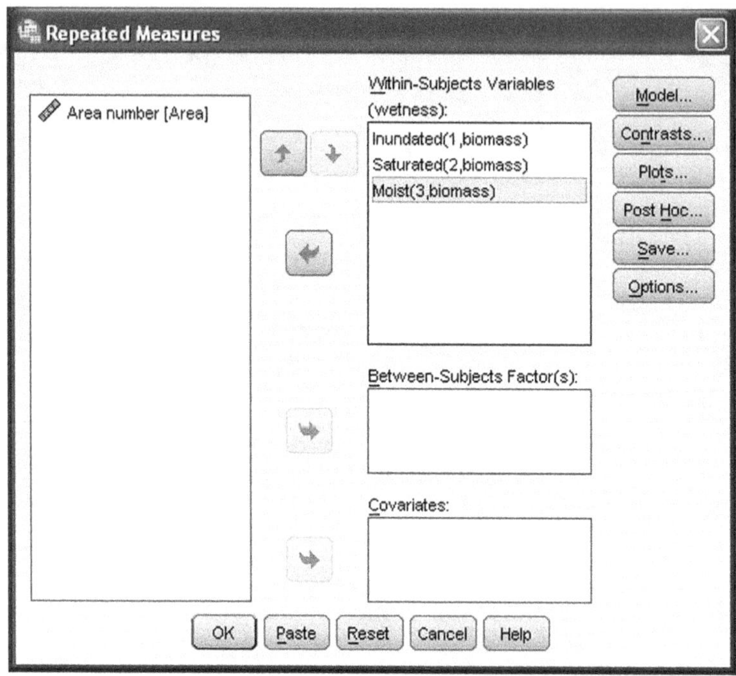

The 'Between-Subjects' box is not needed yet. We will need it when we get to the mixed-design factorial ANOVA, which combines within- and between-subjects factors.

The Covariates box is for variables which are not of interest to the study but which might influence interactions. The extraneous factor would be controlled for in an analysis of covariance (ANCOVA). ANCOVA is discussed at the end of the book. ANCOVA is a controversial procedure; read about it before even thinking of using it.

Within Options, transfer 'wetness' to the 'Display Means for' box on the right. Select the 'Compare main effects' tick-box and set the 'Confidence interval adjustment' to 'Sidak' (discussed soon). Select 'Descriptive statistics' and 'Estimates of effect size'. The significance level box at the bottom refers to analysis of the pairs of conditions ('levels'). Press 'Continue', then 'OK' in the main Repeated Measures dialog box.

The first two output boxes confirm that the data input is correct and provides the basic statistics. (Academic reports commonly cite both the mean and the standard deviation, '*SD*').

Ignore the output on multivariate tests, at this stage and later in the readout. Next comes Mauchly's Test of Sphericity. As well as the usual assumptions for parametric tests, repeated-measures ANOVAs have an assumption of sphericity (equality of the variances between each pair of levels). If the test of sphericity is significant at < .05, the assumption is violated. In this case, however, the 'Sig.' reading of .432 is clearly non-significant. In the event of a significant result, we would then consult the 'Epsilon' figures to the right; this is discussed in detail when the problem arises in the exercise on two-way ANOVA mixed design, towards the end of the chapter.

The main point of the exercise is dealt with by Tests of Within-Subjects Effects. As the sphericity test was non-significant, we read from the top row ('Sphericity Assumed'): $F = 3.706$, Sig. = .045 and Partial Eta Squared = .292.

Analysis of variance calculates how much of the variance derives from independent variables and how much is due to error (error variance). The calculation, the variance divided by the error, is the *F* ratio, referred to in the output as '*F*'. The more the variable's effect outweighs the error, the bigger the *F* ratio and the more likely a significant result. The null hypothesis is that the means of the data groups are all equal.

The repeated-measures ANOVA includes a variance estimate relating to the cases.

Here, we see a critical value of $p < .05$ – the effect is significant. We can reject the null hypothesis that the variances are equal.

If the sphericity test had proved to be significant, we would have read off either the Greenhouse–Geisser or Huyn–Feldt row of figures. The mixed-design ANOVA exercise provides guidance on this.

Partial Eta Squared refers to the effect size, in this case a small one.

EFFECT SIZE AND THE ANALYSIS OF DIFFERENCES

One rule of thumb is that an effect size of 0.2 to 0.5 is small, 0.5 to 0.8 is medium and greater than 0.8 is large.

Ignore the 'Within-subjects contrasts' output.

Pairwise Comparisons

Measure: biomass

(I) wetness	(J) wetness	Mean Difference (I-J)	Std. Error	Sig.[b]	95% Confidence Interval for Difference[b]	
					Lower Bound	Upper Bound
1	2	-.400	3.964	1.000	-11.987	11.187
	3	-9.100*	2.885	.035	-17.531	-.669
2	1	.400	3.964	1.000	-11.187	11.987
	3	-8.700	4.333	.210	-21.366	3.966
3	1	9.100*	2.885	.035	.669	17.531
	2	8.700	4.333	.210	-3.966	21.366

Based on estimated marginal means

*. The mean difference is significant at the .05 level.

b. Adjustment for multiple comparisons: Sidak.

Consulting the Pairwise Comparisons table, we find that the difference between the means of 'Inundated' and 'Moist' provides a *p* value of .035 which is less than the critical value of $p < .05$. Significance is denoted by an asterisk; this would not have appeared had we adjusted our significance expectation to < .01.

The confidence intervals refer, at a 95% estimate, to how broad the ranges of values are likely to be. With larger data sets, this concept is likely to be quite useful for qualifying predictions.

Let us consider briefly the nature of the multiple comparison tests. An adjustment is often made in the case of multiple comparisons of pairs. The more comparisons, the more likely are fluke results, giving us false positives. The Sidak test has been used as the alternative, the Bonferroni test, is nowadays considered to be overly harsh (Rice 1989). However, the Bonferroni in this exercise provides the same *p* value for our significant result and is only slightly increased for the relationship between Moist and Saturated. In many situations, both tests give similar results. The choice of comparison tests is discussed at greater length later in the chapter.

If you had used the default LSD setting, which essentially omits adjustment for statistical flukes, you would still only find one significant result, although at a critical value of $p < .02$. However, while the relationship between Moist and Saturated is still non-significant, we *could* refer to the *p* value of .076 as a possible *trend*. While the statistical adjustments are designed to stop false positives (Type 1 errors), it is quite possible that this small data set has led to a Type 2 error, a false negative.

Here I have considered the LSD result as an exercise. If there had been no clear expectation of conditions being significantly different from each other, then using the LSD result in this situation would simply have been a type of dredging. In this particular case, however, there is a theoretical underpinning: evidence supports the likelihood of varying degrees of wetness affecting plant life (Ellery Mayence *et al.* 2010). For a detailed discussion of the use of multiple comparisons, see the end of this chapter.

Non-parametric version: Friedman

The Friedman test extends the Wilcoxon, and we can add a new condition to our spectroscopy file from the Wilcoxon exercise. We have decided to assess the functionality of three spectroscopy methods.

Table 6.7

		Independent variable: Spectroscopy methods		
		Method A	**Method B**	**Method C**
Dependent variable: Usefulness	Compound 1	4	5	5
	Compound 2	3	3	3
	Compound 3	2	4	2
	Compound 4	4	5	2
	Compound 5	3	5	2
	Compound 6	4	2	2
	Compound 7	3	3	1
	Compound 8	5	4	3
	Compound 9	3	5	2
	Compound 10	4	5	4
	Compound 11	3	5	2
	Compound 12	2	4	3
	Compound 13	2	5	1

DATA ENTRY

If restarting SPSS, choose 'Open an existing data source'. In Variable View, type 'C' in the next row under Name, set Decimal to zero and under Label type 'Method C'. In Data View, you will see a new 'C' column into which you type the Condition C data (leaving the rest unchanged).

ANALYSIS

To examine the basic statistics, use *Analyze/Descriptive Statistics/Frequencies* and press the 'Statistics' button to select the median (mean is also available). Method C is clearly less functional than the others.

Statistics

		A Method	B Method	C Method
N	Valid	13	13	13
	Missing	0	0	0
Median		3.00	5.00	2.00

You can try *Analyze/Nonparametric Tests/Related Samples.* Use the 'Fields' tab to transfer 'Method A', 'Method B' and 'Method C' to the right-hand box, then press 'Run'. We see the Friedman p value as .002, with a significance of $p < .05$. Personally, I find that a little confusing, so we'll use *Analyze/Nonparametric Tests/Legacy Dialogs/K Related Samples* (K means any number above two). The three variables need to be in the right-hand 'Test Variables' box. Ensure that the Friedman test is selected and press 'OK'. Here, you are given the p value of .002, which I would interpret as $p < .01$.

There is a significant overall difference between the three conditions. As the Friedman test, like ANOVA, is what is called an 'omnibus test', only examining overall differences, you may wish to follow up by testing for significance between the pairs, using the Wilcoxon test. The danger of dredging – increasing the likelihood of false positives – suggests that we should multiply our significance levels. One adjustment method is the Bonferroni method, requiring a multiplication by the number of potential tests.

If you run *Analyze/Nonparametric Tests/Legacy Dialogs/Two Related Samples*, you can contrast the pairs.

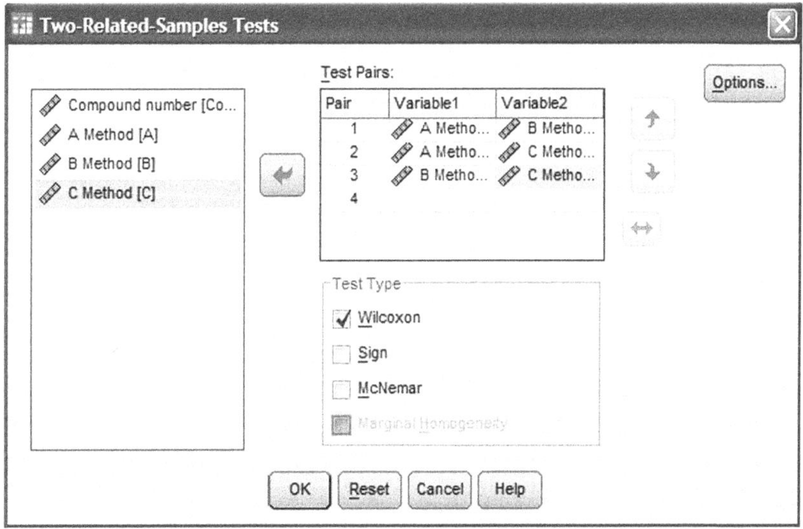

Test Statistics[c]

	B Method - A Method	C Method - A Method	C Method - B Method
Z	-2.092[a]	-2.153[b]	-2.831[b]
Asymp. Sig. (2-tailed)	.036	.031	.005

a. Based on negative ranks.

b. Based on positive ranks.

c. Wilcoxon Signed Ranks Test

Using the Bonferroni method, the *p* values (significance) should become 3 × .036, 3 × .031 and 3 × .005, giving .108, .093 and .015 – only the last pairing, the largest difference, would be seen as significant, $p < .02$.

Some statisticians deem Bonferroni to be harsh. Perhaps we could multiply by the number of pairings minus .5. So we multiply the significance values by 2.5: again, however, only the last of these would be seen as significant, giving .01, again $p < .02$.

For a detailed discussion of multiple comparisons, see the end of the chapter.

THE ALTERNATIVE TO REPEATED-MEASURES ANOVA

We can subject the data from the repeated-measures ANOVA exercise (on the wetlands region) to the Friedman test. This gives a similar result, .025, giving the same standard critical value of $p < .05$.

In the absence of the comparison tests offered by ANOVA, but knowing that we have parametric data (so we do not need to resort to Wilcoxon tests), we can run sets of paired *t* tests to examine relationships between individual pairs of data. Do remember, however, that as previously advised, these post-hoc tests should have their significance levels adjusted somewhat (although see the end of the chapter for more on the subject of multiple comparisons).

Use *Analyze/Compare Means/Paired-Samples* t *Test*, putting all three pairings in the right-hand box. We get the same results as in the ANOVA LSD pairing comparisons. If we use my crude Bonferroni technique and multiply the .012 *p* value for Inundation and Moist (.012 × 3 = .036), we get something very close to the ANOVA Bonferroni output. If my milder method is used, reducing the pairing number by .5 (.012 × 2.5 = .03), the significance is still $p < .05$.

FACTORIAL ANOVA

Factorial analyses of variance examine two or more factors at once. Factorial ANOVA has a dual focus. Like the one-way ANOVA, it examines differences between the levels (conditions) for each factor, referred to as the *main effect*. What distinguishes factorial ANOVA is that it also looks at the *interaction*, the relationship between factors.

Factorial ANOVA is generally used for two-way and occasionally three-way analyses. *Extending ANOVA beyond three factors tends to make interpretation very difficult.*

(It is possible to move completely the other way and apply one-way ANOVA to only two conditions, but a *t* test would suffice for such a purpose.)

Effect size for factorial ANOVA

Clark-Carter (1997) recommends 0.01 as a small effect, 0.06 as medium and 0.14 as large. Kinnear and Gray (2004) extrapolates this to: small < .01, less than 1% of the variance; medium 0.01 to 0.10 (1–10%); large > 0.10 (more than 10% of variance).

Between-subjects two-way ANOVA

The question of whether to use irrigation or fertiliser when improving tree growth has been a subject for statistical investigation (Williams *et al.* 2002). In this (fictional) example, we are also interested in the effects on different types of tree. Each item of data consists of an average from one plot of trees, based on a calibrated satisfaction rating (the dependent variable) with a maximum rating of 10.

Table 6.8

Factors		Tree types		
	Treatment	**Tree type A**	**Tree type B**	**Tree type C**
This space is reserved (for three-way ANOVA)	**Irrigation**	4,5,6,3,7 5,6,7,4,6	3,4,6,1,6 5,7,6,2,4	2,3,5,1,4 6,6,4,1,4
	Fertiliser	6,8,7,8,6 8,9,7,6,8	3,7,7,6,2 6,8,4,2,6	4,6,7,5,1 6,8,3,3,5

DATA ENTRY

In Variable View, create 'Plot', 'Tree', 'Treatment' and 'Rating', the last of these being the dependent variable. The labels would be extended for clarity to something like 'Plot number', 'Tree type', 'Treatment type' and 'Satisfaction rating' for clarity. Adjust decimals to zero. Under 'Values' for Tree and Treatment, add levels (conditions) for the grouping variables, so Tree could have 1 = 'A Tree', 2 = 'B Tree', 3 = 'C Tree'; for Treatment: 1 = 'Irrigation', 2 = 'Fertiliser'.

In Data View, go to the View menu. If the Value Labels toggle is set to 'on' (ticked), the number you type will be converted automatically to the relevant value name. Being able to enter data clearly and easily is of great importance when dealing with factorial combinations.

I suggest that you input the data from the table into columns, so the order is as follows:

Table 6.9

Case	Tree type	Treatment	Rating
1 - 10	(1) A Tree	(1) Irrigation	N
11 - 20	(1) A Tree	(2) Fertiliser	N
21 - 30	(2) B Tree	(1) Irrigation	N
31 - 40	(2) B Tree	(2) Fertiliser	N
41 - 50	(3) C Tree	(1) Irrigation	N
51 - 60	(3) C Tree	(2) Fertiliser	N

(A tip: in practice, you might find it easiest to go to the Tree type column first, type a '1' into the first cell, then copying the data into rest of the first 20 cells. Then type a '2' into the next 20 cells, followed by '3' in the next 20 cells. Then in the Treatment column, alternate 10 number ones and 10 number twos all the way down. Then follow with the values in the boxes, starting with the top left block of data, then the bottom left block, then the top centre block and so on. Then, as in earlier examples, use *Transform/Compute Variable* and $CASENUM to populate the Case column automatically.)

Here is a snapshot of the data if you have followed this format:

	Plot	Tree	Treatment	Rating
28	28	B Tree	Irrigation	6
29	29	B Tree	Irrigation	2
30	30	B Tree	Irrigation	4
31	31	B Tree	Fertiliser	3
32	32	B Tree	Fertiliser	7
33	33	B Tree	Fertiliser	7
34	34	B Tree	Fertiliser	6

Data View | Variable View

ANALYSIS

In *Graphs/Legacy Dialogs/Boxplot*, select the 'Clustered' item, then 'Define'. The dependent variable (Satisfaction rating) goes in the Variable box, with the main grouping variable (Tree type), under 'Category Axis'. The secondary variable (Treatment type) goes in the 'Define Clusters by' box. Click 'OK'.

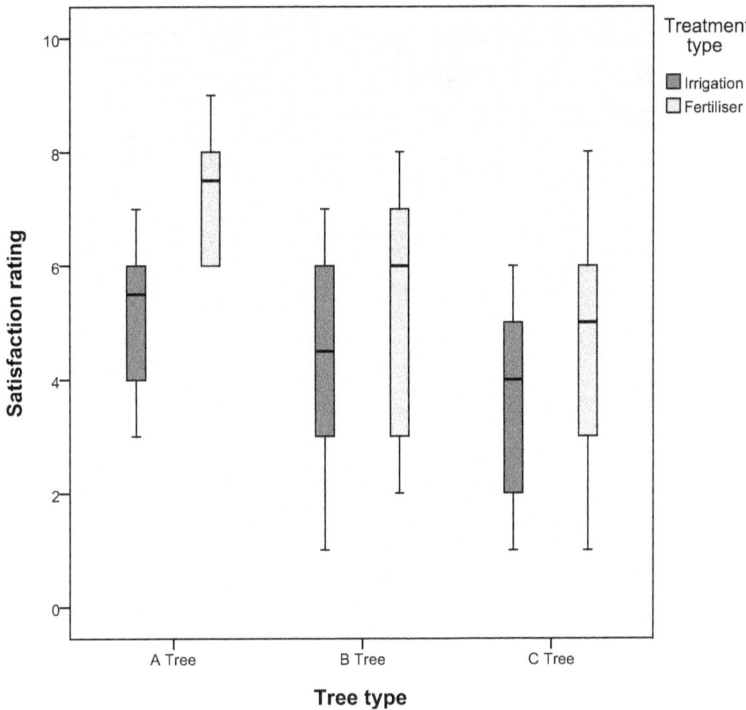

There are no outliers. For each tree type, we see two treatment types, the left side of each box plot represents trees being treated by irrigation, and the right side representing fertiliser treatment. We get the distinct impression that A Tree responds particularly well to fertiliser. It also looks possible, however, that fertiliser works better for all three tree types, but this needs to be checked for significance. It could also be that the different tree types do not differ significantly from each other except in cases where they are treated by fertiliser. We need to test.

Analyze/General Linear Model/Univariate. In the Univariate dialog box, enter Satisfaction rating into the Dependent Variable field; both Tree type and Treatment type go into the Fixed Factor(s) box.

Do not use the Random Factors (rarely used, for when using a random sample of conditions) or Covariate boxes (for variables which may create 'noise', to be discussed at the end of the book when we consider ANCOVA).

Select 'Plots'. Place 'Tree' in the Horizontal Axis box and 'Treatment' into 'Separate Lines'. Then press 'Add' to transfer these to the Plots box. Press 'Continue' to return to the Univariate dialog box.

Select 'Post Hoc' in order to examine the differences between pairs of conditions within the variable (assuming three or more conditions/levels). Transfer 'Tree' to the right-hand window and select 'Tukey', 'Continue' again.

Within 'Options', select 'Descriptive Statistics', 'Estimates of effect size' and 'Homogeneity tests'. Press 'Continue', then 'OK'.

First, check the initial summary to make sure that you are analysing the correct cases (in this exercise, the three tree types have 20 cases each and the treatment types have 30 each).

Then examine the descriptive statistics. Here, you will see that the means differ between each tree type and between treatment types (viewable in the 'Total' row at the bottom).

The Levene test is non-significant; homogeneity is not problematic.

We will look at the next table in some detail.

Tests of Between-Subjects Effects

Dependent Variable:Satisfaction rating

Source	Type III Sum of Squares	df	Mean Square	F	Sig.	Partial Eta Squared
Corrected Model	77.083[a]	5	15.417	4.798	.001	.308
Intercept	1550.417	1	1550.417	482.550	.000	.899
Tree	47.433	2	23.717	7.382	.001	.215
Treatment	25.350	1	25.350	7.890	.007	.127
Tree * Treatment	4.300	2	2.150	.669	.516	.024
Error	173.500	54	3.213			
Total	1801.000	60				
Corrected Total	250.583	59				

a. R Squared = .308 (Adjusted R Squared = .244)

The first two rows are not of interest. 'Tree' and 'Treatment' are the main effects, the interaction being 'Tree × Treatment'. (*F* values are usually reported in academic results.) The differences between the tree types are significant, $p < .002$; the same is true for the treatment categories, $p < .01$. The interaction has a small *F* value and is not significant. (*Adjusted R Squared* is a measure of how well the overall model represents the variance; the nearer to 1, the better.)

So while we know that the tree types themselves differ from each other in how they are rated and also that the treatments are significantly different in their effects, we should not assume a reaction between the two effects (i.e. we have no evidence in this data set that different types of tree react differently to different types of treatment).

The differences between the specific tree types are examined with the Tukey test in the 'Multiple Comparisons' output table. Tree A gets a higher rating than either of the other two tree types ($p < .05$ and $p < .002$). Tree B gets poorer ratings than Tree A (one significance asterisk in the table is adjacent to a negative difference in the means) but is not rated significantly higher than Tree C.

This impression is reinforced when we see the means placed into subsets from the Tukey test. Where means share a subset, the means are not significantly different.

Satisfaction rating

Tukey HSD [a,b]

Tree type	N	Subset	
		1	2
C Tree	20	4.20	
B Tree	20	4.75	
A Tree	20		6.30
Sig.		.599	1.000

Means for groups in homogeneous subsets are displayed.
Based on observed means.
The error term is Mean Square(Error) = 3.213.

a. Uses Harmonic Mean Sample Size = 20.000.

b. Alpha = .05.

According to our (fictional) data set, it would appear that fertilisers are likely to produce superior effects compared to irrigation and that the choice of one treatment or the other is not dependent on the type of tree, i.e. not a matter of 'horses for courses'. Having said that, Tree A clearly responds more positively to fertiliser.

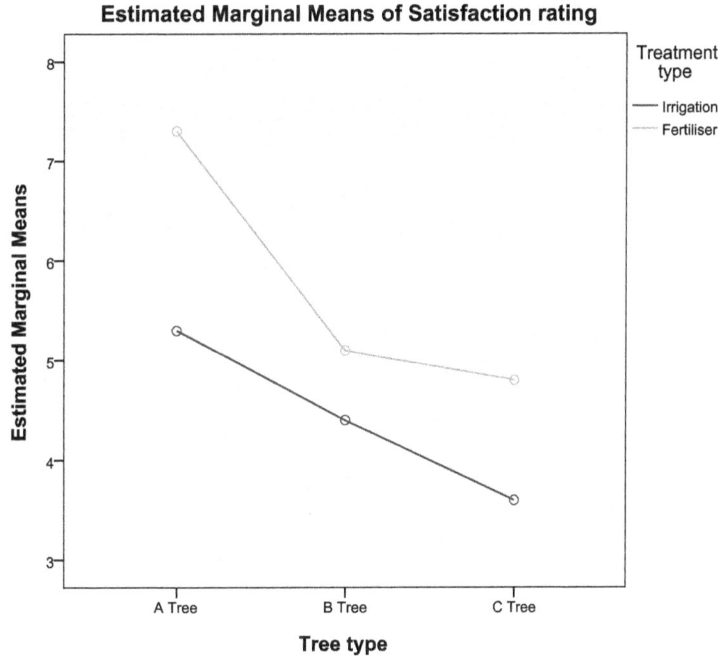

The tree types are on the horizontal axis, with treatment types on the vertical, the upper line representing fertiliser treatment, which produced higher ratings amongst all three tree types.

If the lines were to cross each other or would head towards this if the lines were to be extended, then an interaction would be indicated. This is not the case here. We cannot say with confidence that a particular tree would respond better to one treatment type or another.

More interesting, however, is the position of A Tree on the lower scoring irrigation treatment line. It still has a higher rating under irrigation than the other tree types have even when treated by fertiliser. This tree type grows well under irrigation conditions; depending on circumstances, a grower could decide not to use fertilisers on this particular type of tree.

READING FACTORIAL ANOVA CHARTS

A flat line indicates no difference in conditions across a variable. A line which slopes indicates a main effect, a change between conditions.

If two lines slope but are in parallel, then two main effects would appear to exist but not an interaction between them.

If the lines cross, or would cross if the data was extended, then an interaction is indicated.

As is suggested by the graph previously shown, each graph should be examined carefully to see what it says about the particular data under analysis.

Between-subjects three-way ANOVA

Table 6.10

Factors		Tree types		
Farm	**Treatment**	**Tree type A**	**Tree type B**	**Tree type C**
Farm A	Irrigation	4,5,6,3,7	3,4,6,1,6	2,3,5,1,4
Farm B		5,6,7,4,6	5,7,6,2,4	6,6,4,1,4
Farm A	Fertiliser	6,8,7,8,6	3,7,7,6,2	4,6,7,5,1
Farm B		8,9,7,6,8	6,8,4,2,6	6,8,3,3,5

DATA ENTRY

A new variable, Farm, has been added. Create this in Variable View, providing Values of 1 = Farm A and 2 = Farm B. If you used the previous data input system, then in Data View, you would alternate 5 Farm A ratings and 5 Farm B all the way down the Farm column. So that the whole name appears, I would suggest setting *View/Value Labels* to 'on'. The screenshot shows the first 12 cases.

	Plot	Tree	Treatment	Rating	Farm
1	1	A Tree	Irrigation	4	Farm A
2	2	A Tree	Irrigation	5	Farm A
3	3	A Tree	Irrigation	6	Farm A
4	4	A Tree	Irrigation	3	Farm A
5	5	A Tree	Irrigation	7	Farm A
6	6	A Tree	Irrigation	5	Farm B
7	7	A Tree	Irrigation	6	Farm B
8	8	A Tree	Irrigation	7	Farm B
9	9	A Tree	Irrigation	4	Farm B
10	10	A Tree	Irrigation	6	Farm B
11	11	A Tree	Fertiliser	6	Farm A
12	12	A Tree	Fertiliser	8	Farm A

ANALYSIS

Use the same procedure as in the last exercise, but add 'Farm' to the Fixed Factors box. To save space, I will only refer to output which is additional or rather different from the previous exercise.

Check the Between-Subjects Factors table: you should have 30 Farm A and 30 Farm B ratings. The descriptive statistics indicate higher scores for Farm B than for Farm A; this appears to be the case throughout the table, but we will need to check for significance.

The differences across the Tree types are significant, $p < .005$; Treatment conditions also differ, $p < .01$, with effect sizes of about 22% and 13%.

Differences between the farms proved not to be significant. (If you go to the trouble of separating out the ratings according to Farm provenance, you will still find a non-significant result. A correlational test of this data will in fact show that there is something of a relationship between the two conditions rather than a difference. The variances and the ratings travelled in the same direction, upwards or downwards, despite the differences in score size.)

Non-significance in this particular variant of split-plot design is not to be sneezed at. It rather lends support to the idea that the other results are in fact consistent.

None of the interactions were significant, including the new three-way interaction of Tree, Treatment and Farm.

Within-subjects two-way ANOVA

This test requires the SPSS Advanced Module. You should do the exercise on within-subjects one-way ANOVA before attempting this one.

Three sheep-handling methods are being tested, on each of a flock of 10 sheep. As well as contrasting the methods, we also want to find out if the time of day is relevant. The dependent variable is a rating scale, with 1 as the lowest possible score with the animals being completely calm, to 10 as the highest, denoting considerable distress.

DATA ENTRY

Clarity in how the data is structured is very important. First, separate the data according to the handling method factor, then subdivide it by the second factor, the time factor. Each datum then represents a combination from the factorial structure:

Table 6.11

	Method A (1)		**Method B (2)**		**Method C (3)**	
Sheep	**a.m. (1)**	**p.m. (2)**	**a.m. (1)**	**p.m. (2)**	**a.m. (1)**	**p.m. (2)**
1	6	8	4	5	6	8
2	4	5	3	4	4	4
3	9	8	6	5	8	6
4	7	4	7	6	8	8
5	6	7	6	6	7	6
6	7	8	5	7	6	7
7	5	5	4	3	4	5
8	6	8	4	5	5	7
9	4	3	3	4	5	6
10	6	9	4	6	5	8

Note the order of the columns: 1,1 – 1,2 – 2,1 – 2,2 – 3,1 – 3,2 This will be very important when you transfer variables into the Repeated Measures dialog box.

In Variable View, enter the subdivisions vertically (the 'Measures' field should retain the 'Scale' default):

	Name	Type	Width	Decimals	Label
1	Case	Numeric	8	0	Sheep number
2	Aam	Numeric	8	0	A morning
3	Apm	Numeric	8	0	A afternoon
4	Bam	Numeric	8	0	B morning
5	Bpm	Numeric	8	0	B afternoon
6	Cam	Numeric	8	0	C morning
7	Cpm	Numeric	8	0	C afternoon

The columns in *Data View* appear thus:

	Case	Aam	Apm	Bam	Bpm	Cam	Cpm
1	1	6	8	4	5	6	8
2	2	4	5	3	4	4	4
3	3	9	8	6	5	8	6

Analyze/General Linear Model/Repeated Measures. The dialog box for defining the factors appears first and, as usual with SPSS repeated measures, needs to be handled very carefully.

As illustrated in the within-subjects one-way ANOVA exercise, replace 'factor 1' with a meaningful name for the first factor; all names in this dialog box must be eight or fewer characters and start with a lower case letter. Then enter the number of levels, followed by 'Add'. What we do now, which we did not do in the one-way ANOVA, is to repeat this procedure for the second factor, which should give us the left-hand image. Then type the dependent variable name into the Measure Name box and press 'Add' to get the situation portrayed on the right.

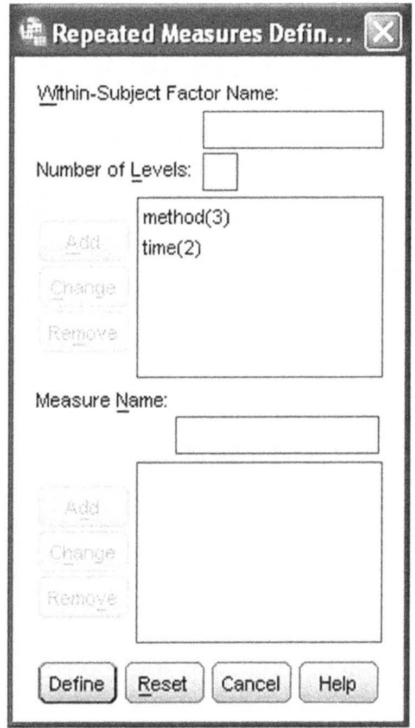

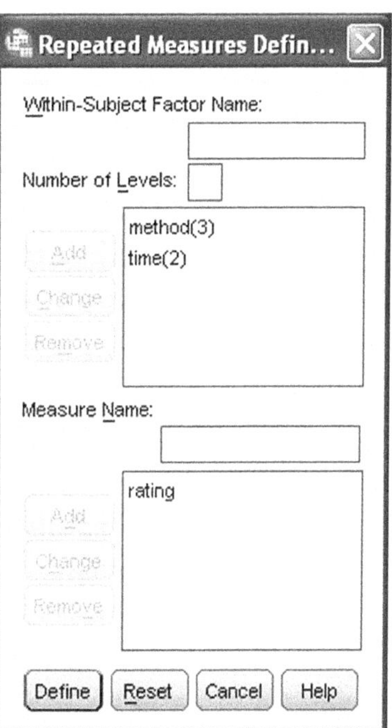

Then press Define, taking us to the Repeated Measures dialog box.

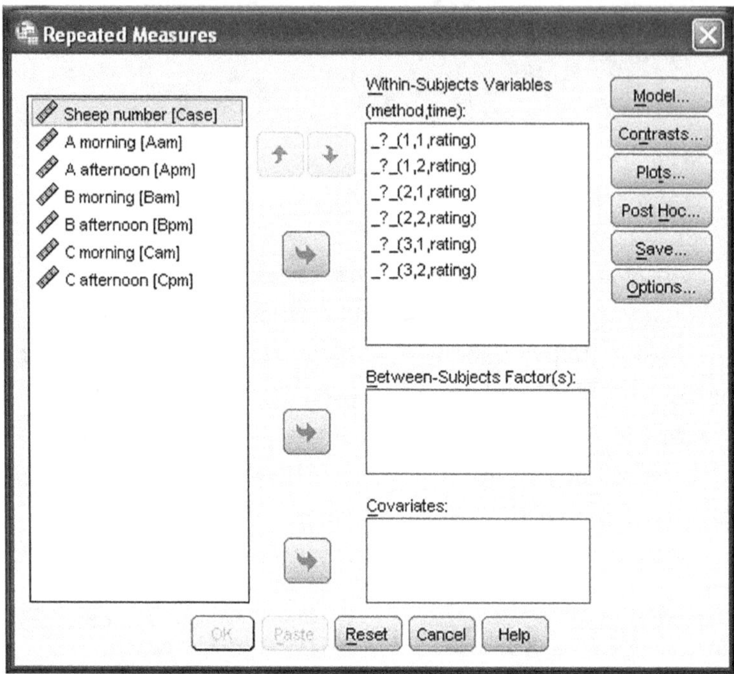

Your newly defined factors (method, time) should appear on the top right. Now you need to be very careful. The transfer of the variables to the right must match our numbering system (e.g. Cpm at the bottom should match '3,2'). You should adopt the practice of transferring variables one by one; block transfers can be erratic, especially with a larger number of variables. The next image shows our newly completed dialog box. The vertical buttons allow changes in order.

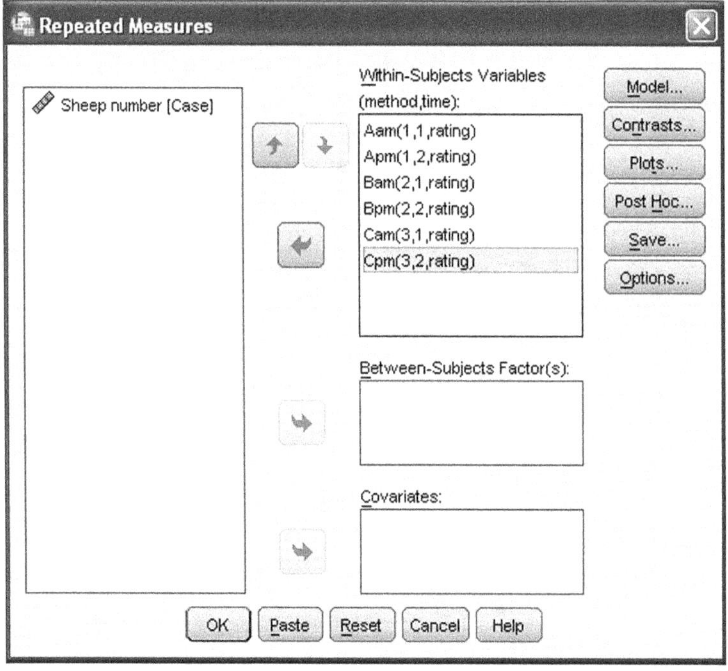

The Between-Subjects box is not used here but will be needed when we run a mixed-design ANOVA.

The Covariates box is for factors which may influence our study but are not of interest in themselves. (Please read my reservations about ANCOVA at the end of the book before considering using this.)

Press the 'Plots' button, placing the factor with the greater number of conditions (levels) onto the horizontal axis, and the other factor onto 'Separate Lines'.

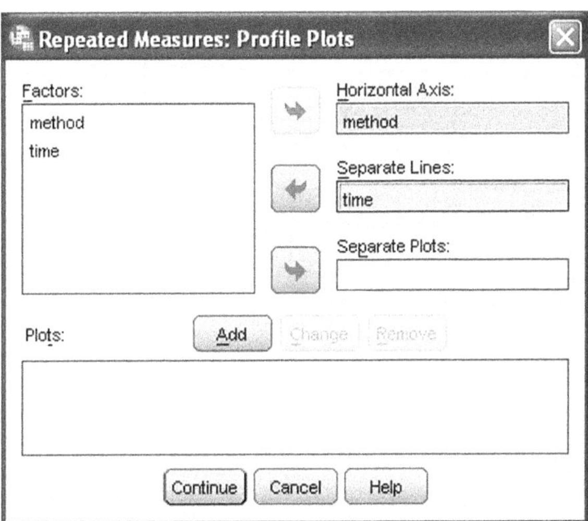

Then click 'Add', which should populate the Plots box:

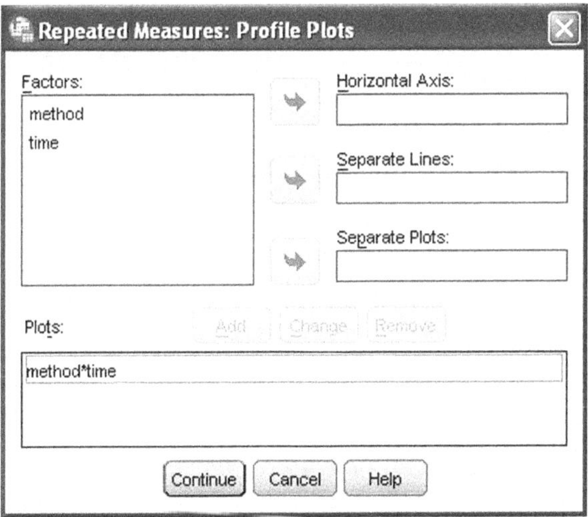

Then press 'Continue'. Go to Options: place 'phase' in the 'Display Means for' box, click the 'Compare main effects' tick-box and choose 'Sidak' as the 'Confidence interval adjustment'. Also select 'Descriptive statistics' and 'Estimates of effect size'. (You could also opt for homogeneity tests, if you have not already checked that your data is suitable for parametric testing.) Press 'Continue'.

Ignore 'Post Hoc', as these tests are not used with repeated measures.

ANALYSIS

Within-Subjects Factors

Measure: rating

method	time	Dependent Variable
1	1	Aam
	2	Apm
2	1	Bam
	2	Bpm
3	1	Cam
	2	Cpm

The first output allows you to check that you have defined the factors correctly. The second output provides the mean and standard deviation (*SD*), which are both usually reported in academic papers. There are rather lower means for 'Bam' and 'Bpm'.

Ignore all output referring to multivariate tests and multivariate contrasts.

The sphericity test is non-significant; the sphericity assumption for repeated measures has not been violated. (There is no test for 'time' as this has only two levels.) In cases where you get a significant sphericity result, read the exercise on mixed ANOVA to see what to do.

'Tests of Within-Subjects Effects' are of central interest. Read the 'sphericity assumed' line. One main effect, phase, appears to be significant, $F = 9.438$, Sig. = .002 (a critical value of $p < .01$) and has a very large effect size, Partial Eta Squared = .512 which accounts for more than half of the variance. The other main effect and the interaction are non-significant.

Ignore the output for 'Tests of Within-Subjects Contrasts' and also for between-subjects effects (irrelevant here).

Output called 'Estimated Marginal Means' shows a difference between Method B (4.850) and the other two handling methods, both of which seem to have quite similar means (6.250 and 6.150 respectively).

The 'Pairwise Comparisons' output shows significant differences between the second method and the other two ($p = .022$; $p = .001$). There is no significant difference between Methods A and C. If the Bonferroni correction had been used instead of the Sidak, the same significance levels would have appeared. This is often the case, but see the mixed design ANOVA exercise for a different outcome and a more detailed discussion.

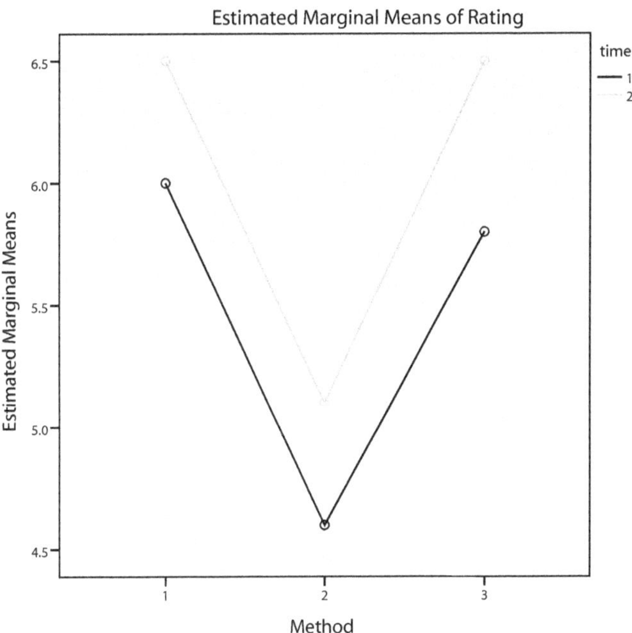

Time number 1 (morning). is the lower of the two lines. The fact that both 'time' lines follow the same route means that the 'handling' effect is a 'global' one. As the lines do not intersect nor do they even tend that way, no interaction is indicated.

It is generally worth examining every factorial ANOVA plot with great care.

In this exercise, it seems that handling method B was significantly more successful in reducing distress in the flock than the other methods.

Within-subjects three-way ANOVA

Sheep can distinguish between familiar and unfamiliar handlers and they do not forget a face (Court *et al.* 2010). So if we think that the individual handler is important, we may decide to split our data further. For the sake of simplicity, let us say that we are using two handlers, one with considerable experience and empathy, the other a novice of unknown quality. To contain the 'handler' factor, we would change Variable View. Instead of having 'Aam', 'Bam', we would have factors like 'AamExpert', 'AamNovice', etc. Similarly, the input for SPSS would be extended and great care would be needed.

Table 6.12

Method A (1)				**Method B (2)**				**Method C (3)**			
a.m. (1)		p.m. (2)		a.m. (1)		p.m. (2)		a.m. (1)		p.m. (2)	
E (1)	N (2)	E (1)	N (2)	E (1)	N (2)	E (1)	N (2)	E (1)	N (2)	E (1)	N (2)

We have a new rhythm: 1,1,1 – 1,1,2 – 1,2,1 – etc.

Mixed-design two-way ANOVA

Mixed designs require the SPSS Advanced Module.

We want to find out how effective over a short period of time are three different types of ultraviolet treatment for patients with moderate to severe psoriasis. As each person with the skin disorder tends to react differently from each other, a within-subjects design seems to make sense in terms of the patients; each year, the same people try out a different type of therapy (the order being randomised to avoid potential order effects).

However, we also want to see if the effectiveness varies according to whether or not the patients attribute their conditions to stressful environments; as some say it does and some say it does not, this will be the between-subjects part of our mixed design. The (fictional) data is the extent of skin clearance over a fixed period of time expressed as a percentage.

DATA ENTRY

This is the design structure:

Table 6.13

	UV light A	UV light B	UV light C
Stress reported			
Stress not reported			

In Variable View, after the case number, one row represents the grouping category, with the following three adjacent rows representing treatments to be undertaken by all the patients.

	Name	Type	Width	Decimals	Label	Values
1	Case	Numeric	8	0	Patient number	None
2	Category	Numeric	8	0	Stress category	{1, stress re...
3	UVA	Numeric	8	0	UV A	None
4	UVB	Numeric	8	0	UV B	None
5	UVC	Numeric	8	0	UV C	None

The grouping category's 'Measure' should be set to 'Nominal'. For the requisite values, I suggest 1 = stress reported and 2 = stress not reported.

	Case	Category	UVA	UVB	UVC
1	1	stress repo...	80	82	78
2	2	stress repo...	65	67	64
3	3	stress repo...	50	58	45
4	4	stress repo...	68	69	70
5	5	stress repo...	63	66	63
6	6	stress repo...	57	56	58
7	7	stress not ...	84	83	84
8	8	stress not ...	70	75	71
9	9	stress not ...	70	76	72
10	10	stress not ...	57	62	58
11	11	stress not ...	46	60	42
12	12	stress not ...	55	64	51

The image shows the completed Data View.

ANALYSIS

Analyze/Descriptive Statistics/Explore can be used to check for extreme values.

Analyze/General Linear Model/Repeated Measures. In Within-Subject Factor Name, replace 'factorl' with an overall variable name such as 'uvtypes' (no more than eight letters, lower case and not the same word as any previously chosen variable names). The number of levels for tests will be 3. 'Add' should place 'uvtypes(3)' in the main box. In the Measure Name box, type a name like 'score' for the dependent variable. Again, 'Add'.

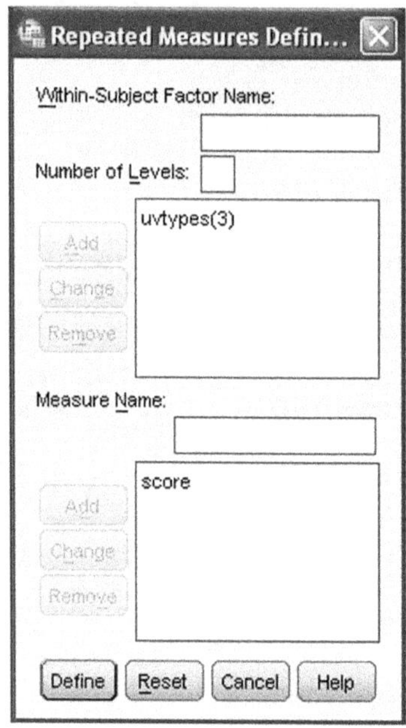

Then 'Define'.

In the Repeated Measures dialog box, transfer UVA, UVB and UVC to the Within-Subjects Variables box. Place 'Category' into the Between-Subjects Factor box.

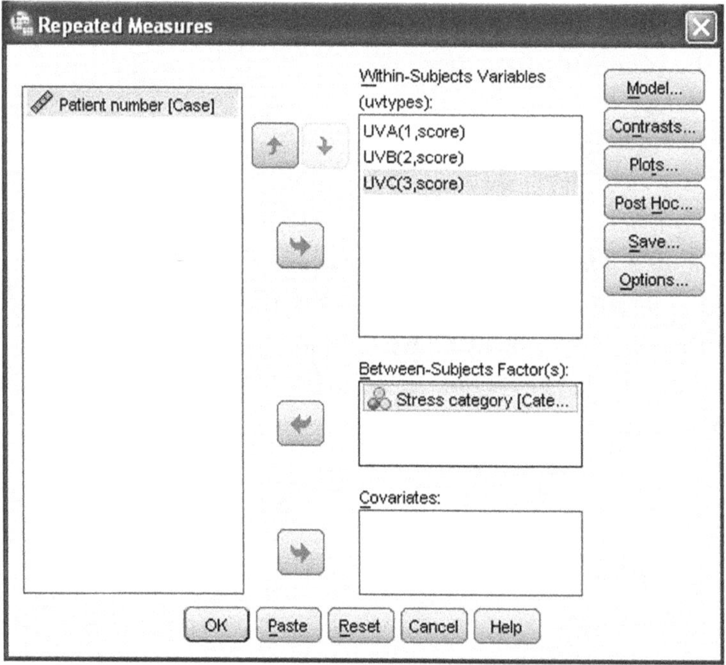

In 'Plots', place 'uvtypes' in 'Horizontal Axis' as it has the most levels and Category in 'Separate Lines', clicking 'Add' to transfer uvtypes*Category to the field at the bottom. Press 'Continue'.

In 'Options', do the following: Place 'uvtypes' in the 'Display Means for' box. Tick 'Compare main effects' and select 'Sidak' for 'Confidence interval adjustment'. Select 'Descriptive statistics' and 'Estimates of effect size'. Press 'Continue'.

'Post-hoc' tests are not required as there are only two levels for the between-subjects category (Category); had there been more, you would have selected the Tukey check box to examine the levels in pairs. Press 'Continue', then 'OK'.

Mauchly's Test of Sphericity

Measure: score

Within Subjects Effect	Mauchly's W	Sig.	Epsilon		
			Greenhouse-Geisser	Huynh-Feldt	Lower-bound
uvtypes	.161	.000	.544	.620	.500

Houston, we have a problem. A significant Mauchly test indicates that the sphericity assumption for repeated measures has been utterly violated. So we need to consider reading from adjusted values. We will return to this output box quite soon.

Tests of Within-Subjects Effects

Measure: score

Source		Mean Square	F	Sig.	Partial Eta Squared
uvtypes	Sphericity Assumed	93.528	8.988	.002	.473
	Greenhouse-Geisser	172.036	8.988	.011	.473
	Huynh-Feldt	150.907	8.988	.008	.473
	Lower-bound	187.056	8.988	.013	.473
uvtypes * Category	Sphericity Assumed	14.083	1.353	.281	.119
	Greenhouse-Geisser	25.905	1.353	.274	.119
	Huynh-Feldt	22.723	1.353	.277	.119
	Lower-bound	28.167	1.353	.272	.119
Error(uvtypes)	Sphericity Assumed	10.406			
	Greenhouse-Geisser	19.140			
	Huynh-Feldt	16.789			
	Lower-bound	20.811			

We must ignore the 'Sphericity Assumed' line, selecting an adjustment instead. Some researchers always use Huynh–Feldt, others always Greenhouse–Geisser. My advice is to return to the Mauchly's Test of Sphericity output box. If the Epsilon statistic for Huynh–Feldt is greater than .75, use Huynh–Feldt; otherwise use Greenhouse–Geisser. In this case, the Epsilon value is .620, so we should use Greenhouse–Geisser. So when we return to the effects output, our 'uvtypes' variable is .011 ($p < .02$), rather than the smaller critical value according to the usual reading.

We are not concerned with the interaction, which is clearly non-significant.

In the 'Tests of Between-Subjects Effects', the effect for the stress reporting category is also non-significant.

The 'Estimated Means' tells us that the second UV treatment is more effective than the others.

Pairwise Comparisons

Measure: score

(I) uvtypes	(J) uvtypes	Mean Difference (I-J)	Std. Error	Sig. [b]	95% Confidence Interval for Difference[b]	
					Lower Bound	Upper Bound
1	2	-4.417*	1.186	.012	-7.809	-1.024
	3	.750	.743	.708	-1.374	2.874
2	1	4.417*	1.186	.012	1.024	7.809
	3	5.167*	1.801	.049	.015	10.318
3	1	-.750	.743	.708	-2.874	1.374
	2	-5.167*	1.801	.049	-10.318	-.015

Based on estimated marginal means

*. The mean difference is significant at the .05 level.

b. Adjustment for multiple comparisons: Sidak.

The Pairwise Comparisons output, according to the Sidak adjustment, indicates a significant difference between the first and second conditions at p value .012, critical value $p < .02$, likewise the second and third conditions at .049, $p < .05$.

If the Bonferroni adjustment is used, however, the relationship between the third and first condition is .050, which is not smaller than .05.

You will find a detailed discussion a little later in the chapter about possible choices of adjustment tests. At this point, it is reasonable to say that many researchers use the Bonferroni as the traditional default, but modern commentators consider Bonferroni too harsh (e.g. Rice 1989), with the Sidak test as the usual alternative for within-subjects pairings.

In this case, I feel that the serious violation of an assumption for repeated-measures tests makes a conservative test more appropriate. However, given the closeness to significance, it may be well worth citing both tests and recommending a replication. Also, readers who are given both sets of readings can arrive at their own conclusions.

Mixed-design three-way ANOVA: 2 between-subjects and 1 within-subjects

Mixed designs require the SPSS Advanced Module.

We may want to see whether or not the different ultraviolet treatments affect males and females differently. So we have light treatment as the within-subjects variable and both stress and gender as the between-subjects variables.

In *Variable View*, we have the following variables:

* Case Gender Stress UVA UVB UVC.

  Values need to be assigned to the gender grouping variable as well as to 'stress'.

In this variant, when you get to the Repeated Measures dialog box, there will only be one variable at the top as the Within-Subjects Variable: 'uvtypes'. UVA, UVB and UVC will be transferred to the right-hand window. However, two variables are to be transferred to the Between-Subjects Factor box, the stress and gender categories.

Mixed-design three-way ANOVA: 2 within-subjects and 1 between-subjects

Mixed designs require the SPSS Advanced Module.

This time, we'll have a different variant of our light treatment. We could choose to provide two different types of emollient cream to be used during treatment. As all patients would try both, we now have two within-subject variables, UV treatment and cream. The different attitudes to the concept of stress comprise the between-subject variable. In addition to the variables 'Case' and 'Stress', we have to enter six new variables into *Variable View*, combining treatment type (UVA) with cream (c).

An example of the structure is shown here as if transposed into Data View (using imaginary figures):

Table 6.14

Case	Category	UVAc1	UVAc2	UVBc1	UVBc2	UVCc1	UVCc2
12	stress not	80	83	86	88	81	82

In Within-Subject Factor Name, replace factor1 with 'uvtypes', with 3 for the number of levels. Then 'Add'. As in the Two-Way ANOVA Repeated Measures, 'define' twice, the second time for 'cream' but with only '2' for levels.

Transfer UVAc1, UVAc2, UVBc1, UVBc2, UVCc1 and UVCc2 to the Within-Subjects Variables box in the Repeated Measures dialog box. Take great care with the sequence. Make sure that 'Within-Subjects Variables' at the top says [uvtype, cream] and that the transfer to the right-hand box is as follows:

- UVAc1[1,1,score]
- UVAc2[1,2,score]
- UVBc1[2,1,score]
- UVBc2[2,2,score]
- UVCc1[3,1,score]
- UVCc2[3,2,score].

Then, as with the mixed-design two-way ANOVA, the stress category goes in the Between-Subjects Factor box.

MULTIPLE COMPARISONS

As mentioned previously, the null hypothesis for analysis of variance is that the means of the data groups are all equal. If the null hypothesis for ANOVA is rejected, we are still unable to determine which of the means differ significantly. It is possible to use a series of *t* tests to examine similarities between individual conditions (levels) of variables, but the greater the number of tests, the likelier we are to encounter Type 1 errors (assuming significance when the null hypothesis should be accepted).

The notion of *planned tests* is not controversial. If certain variable pairings are theoretically important (before data is collected), then pairwise testing is as acceptable as overall effects.

Post-hoc tests, however, are controversial (Games 1971; Sato 1996). These are conducted after significance is found in an ANOVA (dredging pairings in the event of non-significance is a complete no-no). If we accept post hoc tests, then we prefer specialist tests to multiple *t* tests, as they make adjustments for multiple pairings.

The suggestions given below are not definitive and reflect a wide range of opinion within the community of statistical test users. You should always report whichever formulation you use and how it was applied.

One view that is rarely aired these days is that we should be satisfied with the overall effects offered by the ANOVA and eschew all multiple comparisons (Fisher 1935). There is little opposition, however, to the use of planned tests. Theoretical justification should precede data collection. A variation of this is that specialist adjustments are just plain wrong in planned tests and that straightforward *t* tests should be used.

The author is rather inclined to an intermediate view, that post-hoc tests may suggest new hypotheses for investigation, but that their results should be interpreted with considerable scepticism. If one is investigating factors, then that is not the same as examining their constituents. Individual test results could be statistical artefacts or, perhaps more likely, may not have the same theoretical underpinning as the main subject of study.

It has to be said, though, that post-hoc tests are commonly used and analysed. This being the case, here are a few of the strategies suggested by various commentators. As you develop as a researcher, you may form your own views on which (if any) of these make the most sense.

Most of the strategies are based upon how 'conservative' (strict) or otherwise the tests are. Conservative tests are somewhat more likely to lead to Type 2 errors (rejecting significant results), while 'liberal' ones may succumb to Type 1 (accepting a result when the null hypothesis should be accepted).

Between-subjects tests

The Scheffe and Bonferroni tests are generally considered to be the most conservative. Then comes the Tukey. The Dunnet is considered more liberal, then the Duncan, with LSD (least square difference) being the most liberal (Dallal 2001, an interesting internet page on multiple comparisons).

One strategy comprises a combination of Tukey and Fisher's LSD (Dallal 2001). A significant result according to the Tukey test should be accepted as significant. A non-significant result according to LSD should be considered non-significant (remembering that LSD is a very liberal test). If LSD is significant, but Tukey is not, the differences should be viewed as open to further investigation.

Another strategy is to test only the conditions you think are important, using the Tukey test (Dallal 2001).

Use Tukey for larger numbers of conditions and Bonferroni for fewer conditions (Field 2009).

Use the Bonferroni (and perhaps also Scheffe) for unplanned comparisons, a conservative anti-dredging method; for planned comparisons, use the Tukey (Kleinbaum *et al.* 2008).

Use a batch of tests and choose the one with the lowest critical value (Howell 2011).

The Tukey is the most popular (Tsoumakas *et al.* 2005). The default in this book has been to test all conditions with Tukey, having limited the number of ANOVA variables to those which are meaningful within the scope of the research.

Within-subjects tests

The Bonferroni is nowadays considered rather harsh (Rice 1989), although several texts still use it (e.g. Kinnear and Gray 2004). The default in this book is the Sidak. On the other hand, when I had serious doubts about the data, I felt that the more conservative Bonferroni was sensible. In an uncertain case like this, it seems reasonable to report both test results in order to allow readers to reach their own conclusions. In many cases, of course, the results of the two tests do not differ greatly.

Another strategy is to use both tests when examining relatively few pairings and report the lowest result. I personally think that if you use two you should report two.

The real problem tends to be large numbers of pairings. In my opinion it is best to restrict the number of pairings based on reasonable theoretical grounds. This would be better than trawling for unexpected results.

Effect discovery versus treatment choice

Hilton and Armstrong (2006) in an interesting internet article say that 'In many circumstances, different post-hoc tests may lead to the same conclusions and which of the tests is actually used is often a matter of fashion or personal taste. However, each test addresses the statistical problems in a unique way.' They suggest that test usage should be based upon the purpose of the investigation.

If we want to be as sure as possible of whether or not a treatment has an effect, we should choose a conservative test. If we are choosing between different treatments, then a liberal test is less likely to miss an effect.

Choices according to the type of data

Another website article (SSTARS 2011) recommends different comparison tests according to the type of data being analysed. This article is not the easiest of reads, however.

DISCUSSION POINT

The use of post-hoc tests, and also the debate over whether or not to use ANCOVA (discussed at the end of the book), raises some points about our mental habits, both within research and, I would suggest, in everyday life. One is the adoption of technology not on its merits but because we can. Another is the use of software that is referred to as 'powerful', especially when we are not told in what way such a thing is powerful (ok, in the case of tests, it generally means more likely to find an effect). There is also a tendency to see complexity as a virtue, or perhaps to see simplicity as naivety. Yet a further mental habit is to choose ways of thinking because of perceived popularity or the example of respected users. (I shall now make you happier by going to live in a cave.)

This table of tests of difference is not exhaustive, but aims to provide a general guide. **Do remember that there are assumptions to be made about the data before using parametric tests: continuous data, a normal distribution, homogeneity of variance (when samples are of different sizes) and, in repeated-measures ANOVA, sphericity. The diagnostic tests cited in the table should be consulted when considering the use of parametric tests.**

Table 6.15

N.B. *Non-parametric tests can be used with 'parametric' data.*

Design	Test	Conditions	Data
Same or paired subjects	Wilcoxon Paired *t* test Friedman Within-subjects one-way ANOVA Within-subjects factorial ANOVA	2 2 3 or more 3 or more 2 or more, two or more factors	Non-parametric Parametric Non-parametric Parametric Parametric
Different subjects	Mann–Whitney Unpaired *t* test Kruskal–Wallis Between-subjects one-way ANOVA Between-subjects factorial ANOVA	2 2 3 or more 3 or more 2 or more, two or more factors	Non-parametric Parametric Non-parametric Parametric Parametric
Mixed design	Mixed-design factorial ANOVA	2 or more, two or more factors	Parametric
Diagnostic tests for normal distribution	Shapiro–Wilk Kolmogorov–Smirnov	Less than 50 cases Larger numbers	Any data, to see if suitable for parametric tests
Diagnostic test for homogeneity of variance	Levene test		Any data, to see if suitable for parametric tests
Diagnostic test for sphericity	Mauchly's test		Repeated-measures ANOVA

CHAPTER 7

Frequency of observations

On many occasions, we do not deal with measurable data, neither 'scale' nor ordinal. Instead, we have frequencies, counts of observations. While these may be natural observations, such as the number of trout found in one setting as opposed to another, the sources of such data are not always so obvious.

This sort of study is sometimes known as categorical, sometimes as qualitative. However, some users of the term 'qualitative research' mean by this that their data is unquantifiable.

When people interview others or produce other 'qualitative' information, the information gained from such sources often appears to be unquantifiable. People have different opinions about a potential energy source. Minerals fall into different categories according to size or constituent elements. Different categories of situation or behaviour emerge from records of industrial accidents.

Different category memberships are not necessarily better or weightier than others, so the data is *nominal*. However, we may count the *frequency* of occurrence within each category and use frequencies in statistical analysis.

Data must be both *exclusive* and *exhaustive*: each observation is allocated to one category and all observations from a sample must be allocated.

In general, the statistical analyses in this chapter compare what is observed with what may be predicted. Using statistical jargon, calculations contrast the *observed frequencies*, the actual sample, with the *expected frequencies*, also known as *predicted frequencies*.

The null hypothesis may be rejected if the observed and expected frequencies are shown to be significantly different.

It should be noted that the 'expected frequencies' could be random, with equal chances of observations going into any of the given categories. They could also be set to a ratio (such a situation will become clear when we see the Mendelevian examples in the Chi-square goodness of fit tests).

In the case of a random model, the rejection of the null hypothesis, a significant test result, is likely to mean that the categorisation of observations departs from chance. In the case of a ratio, the upholding of the null hypothesis (lack of a significant result) heralds similarity with the expected model; a significant difference would mean that the ratio of the observations (e.g. genetic predisposition) represents a different model.

Different approaches to prediction have implications for our use of p values. Generally, a two-tailed p value is the correct choice. A one-tailed result should be used only if there is a weighty theoretical reason for one classification to be predictably more numerous (not just 'I always felt that was more likely').

DICHOTOMIES: THE BINOMIAL TEST

We will start with a dichotomous event: essentially 'heads or tails'. For example, this test can be used to find out if, during randomised trials, more patients prefer one drug to another (Armitage and Berry 1994).

If we observe 30 cases and find that 17 patients are happier with the effects of Drug A and 13 prefer Drug B, a statistical test is unlikely to find a significant difference between the observed 17:13 and the predicted random value of 15:15.

For this test to be used properly, the probability of one condition or the other – success or failure, if you like – must remain the same throughout: 50:50.

Data entry

RAW DATA INPUT

This is usually for small samples.

In Variable View, name one variable, for example 'drug'. Set the Measure field to 'Nominal' and Decimal to '0'. Click the dotted area to the right of the Value cell. The Value Labels dialog box requires a 1 in the value field and 'Drug A' in the label field, followed by 'Add'. Repeat this with 2 and 'Drug B'. Press 'OK'.

Then type in the data, using only the chosen values (here, 1 and 2) in one Data View column. (If you toggle *View/Value Labels*, you will see the label values instead of the input numbers.)

	drug
1	1
2	2
3	1
4	2
5	2
6	2
7	2
8	1
9	2
10	2
11	1
12	2

Analyze/Nonparametric Tests/Legacy Dialogs/Binomial (simpler than *Analyze/Nonparametric Tests/One Sample*, which does the same job). Transfer the variable 'drug' to the Test Variable List. *Leave the small 'Test Proportion' setting at 0.50 (i.e. 50:50).* Click 'OK' to see the test results (here, non-significant).

SUMMARY DATA INPUT

For larger amounts of data, or data in subsets, it will probably be easier to type in **frequencies**, just one number representing an entire category. One option for data entry is *Analyze/Descriptive Statistics/Frequencies*; another is *Analyze/Descriptive Statistics/Crosstabs.*

Create a variable in Variable View, for example 'drug'. Again, use the Value column, 1 = 'Drug A' and 2 = 'Drug B'. Create a second variable, 'frequency' (again, 'Decimals' set to zero). In Data View, the values – here, 1 and 2 – go under the 'drug' heading and the number of observations per value goes under the frequency heading. For 13 against 17 observations, from a total of 30, we enter the following:

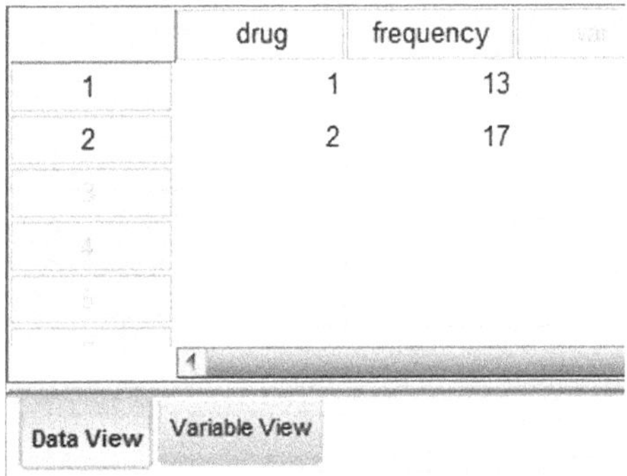

Most important: Data/Weight Cases. Press the 'Weight Cases by' button and transfer 'frequency' to the Frequency Variable box. Then 'OK'.

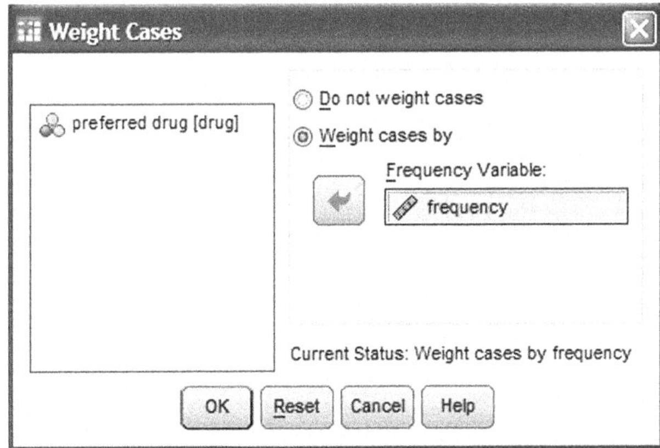

Analysis

Analyze/Nonparametric Tests/Legacy Dialogs/Binomial. Transfer the variable 'drug' to the Test Variable List. *Leave the small 'Test Proportion' setting at 0.50 (i.e. 50:50).* Click 'OK' to see the test results (here, non-significant).

Let us take our example of 30 people deciding if they prefer the effects of Drug A or Drug B. Firstly, out of interest, go to Data View and enter 15 for each condition – a 50/50 scenario:

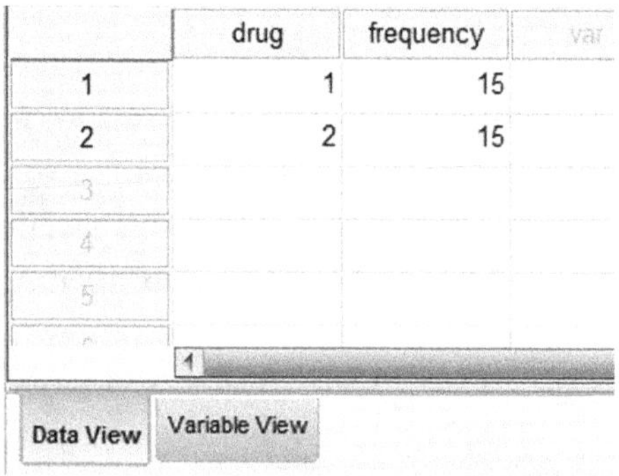

	drug	frequency	var
1	1	15	
2	2	15	
3			
4			
5			

Data View | Variable View

Binomial Test

		Category	N	Observed Prop.	Test Prop.	Asymp. Sig. (2-tailed)
preferred drug	Group 1	Drug A	15	.50	.50	1.000[a]
	Group 2	Drug B	15	.50		
	Total		30	1.00		

a. Based on Z Approximation.

This should be your test result, $p = 1$, the expectation for a 50:50 result, which is made explicit in the Observed Proportions cell.

If you try out the 17:13 scenario, you should read $p = 0.585$, still non-significant. If you enter the reverse, with 13 above and 17 below, the result will be the same, the result being the other side of the coin.

Another example is a survey question. Let us say that a community has already ruled out the idea of sending its waste elsewhere. Respondents have a choice: either dump it in a landfill or burn it in an incinerator. There are just two possible cases, with no abstaining and no voting for both. As with all the examples in this chapter, 'observations' are both exhaustive and exclusive.

Out of 100 respondents, 67 preferred landfill, with 33 preferring the incineration option. So, with frequencies of 67 and 33, we get a test reading of .001 two-tailed.

REPEATED DICHOTOMIES: THE MCNEMAR TEST

Let us imagine that members of the public are invited to give their impressions of a new energy project. Their responses are gathered both before and after a debate involving a panel of experts.

The basic conditions for using this test is that both conditions, pre- and post-, must use categorical data and must be related to each other (correlated). Essentially, the test deals with *paired responses.*

The McNemar test is often used in medicine. One real life example was the monitoring of children at the ages of 12 and then 14 to see if they were liable to bad colds (Bland 2000). Another use is the testing for a particular symptom within a sample of individuals before and after a particular drug has been administered. In both cases, there will be two sets of dichotomies, each with a count of individuals.

For the debate, we could count 'for' and 'against' both before and after the panel had discussed the energy project. For the children aged 12, we would count the number within two categories, 'vulnerable' and 'non-vulnerable'; this would be repeated at age 14. In the drug treatment example, we would have pre- and post-treatment tests with the categories of positive and negative symptoms, as in the table (with imaginary frequencies for 100 patients):

Table 7.1

	Dosage phase	
Symptom status	**Pre-drug**	**Post-drug**
Positive	60	35
Negative	40	65

Note that as these are paired responses, *the numbers in the pre- and post-data sets must be the same.*

Raw data input

If we want to enter data directly, we want two columns of data, with category numbers, looking like this:

	Before	After
1	1	1
2	1	1
3	1	1
4	1	2
5	2	2
6	2	2

Analyse/Descriptive Statistics/Crosstabs. One variable goes into 'Rows', the other into 'Columns'. Then press the 'Statistics' tab and select 'McNemar'. Press 'Continue' and 'OK'.

Summary data input

To enter the frequencies directly, create two variables in Variable View for category names, adjust the Type to 'String' (which automatically changes the Measure type to 'nominal'). Also create a 'Frequency' variable, 'Decimals' adjusted to zero.

	Name	Type	Width	Decimals
1	Before	String	8	0
2	After	String	8	0
3	Frequency	Numeric	8	0
4				

Data/Weight Cases. Select 'Weight cases by'. Place 'Frequency' in the Frequency Variable box. Then 'OK'.

So when you type in frequencies in Data View,

	Before	After	Frequency
1	Yes	Yes	20
2	Yes	No	2
3	No	No	16
4	No	Yes	12

these will be used by the cross-tabulation. Instead of Yes and No, you could have Vulnerable versus Resistant, Present and Absent for symptoms, etc.

Analysis

Analyse/Descriptive Statistics/Crosstabs. Place one variable (e.g. Before) in Rows, the other (e.g. After) in Columns, select the 'Statistics' tab, then choose McNemar. Press 'Continue' and 'OK'. After checking the case summary to ensure that the frequencies are correct, look at the data cross-tabulation and then the McNemar significance statistic of .013, $p < .02$ two-tailed. The 'Before' and 'After' conditions are significantly different. (Ignore the SPSS data warning; if you have checked the data summary and it is correct, then this is just SPSS looking at the summary data as if it were raw data.)

MORE THAN TWO CONDITIONS: CHI-SQUARE GOODNESS OF FIT TEST

During a wave of food poisoning in our local area, we have examined the remains of food thought to be infected by botulism. We want to see if it is true that botulism is most likely to be transmitted via vegetables. We have also been told that fish comes second in the botulism race, with meat and dairy products constituting a minority of botulism cases (Bakalar 2003).

Table 7.2

Vegetable	Fish	Meat/Dairy	Total
80	42	28	150

(A methodological point: if a fourth category had relatively few members, the all too clear difference in the frequency count would distort the test. These observations may be excluded if the rationale is clear and recorded for future scrutiny. Such a rationale does not include 'getting significance'!)

Data entry

Create two variables in Variable View, 'Food' and 'Frequency'. The 'Food' variable requires three levels, with 'Values' set to 1 = Vegetable, 2 = Fish and 3 = Meat or Dairy. In Data View, the data should look something like this:

	Food	Frequency
1	1	80
2	2	42
3	3	28

Data/Weight Cases. 'Frequency' is used as the transfer variable; so the Frequency variable will be used as the criteria (the data being measured).

Analysis

Analyze/Nonparametric Tests/Legacy Dialogs/Chi-square. Transfer the 'Food' variable to the Test Variable List.

Food type

	Observed N	Expected N	Residual
Vegetable	80	50.0	30.0
Fish	42	50.0	-8.0
Meat or ...	28	50.0	-22.0
Total	150		

You will see that the Chi-square calculation compares the observed count with the expected count, which is the essence of Chi-square. The expected count is a calculated random figure: each category is expected to hold 50 members, the expected frequencies representing the total of 150 divided by the 3 conditions. The differences from the observed frequencies are large, especially between 'Vegetable' and its expected value. (In some studies, you may want to change the 'Expected Values' in the dialog box from 'All categories equal' to specified values. An obvious example, pertaining to genetics, will be considered later in the chapter.)

We next see the test statistics: Chi-square is a very large 28.96, with a p value of .000, the critical value being $p < .0005$ – highly significant differences. (At the bottom of the output, we are reminded that Chi-square calculations generally require frequencies of at least 5 per cell.) So we can easily reject the null hypothesis of random classification.

A further example would be an opinion poll. Asked which problem is the *worst* (note the exclusivity of the classification), 105 Londoners gave the following (imaginary) responses: Crime = 35; Global warming = 37; Immigration = 33. (Candidates for a fourth or fifth category might include bankers and media tycoons.) The expected frequency is 35 per category (105/3). The observed categories are all close to the expected frequencies and, sure enough, any difference is insignificant; $p = 0.892$. Security at home will be stepped up, with tougher immigration laws, as the weather becomes more erratic and the tides rise ...

An important methodological point needs to be made about the use of this test. Significance merely indicates that we must reject a hypothesis of non-preference. It does not demonstrate that one particular choice is the strongest.

If we wanted to examine differences more finely, one option would be to create a dichotomy, making the strongest option 'Option A' and placing all the other frequencies into one category, 'Option B'; you would then return to the binomial test. If we return to our food poisoning example – the summary data method would make for quicker data entry (see the binomial test exercise) – make 1 = 'Vegetable' as one value of a variable (e.g. 'Food') and 2 = 'Other food' as the second. On the 'Frequency' variable, 'Vegetable' would have a count of 80 as before, with 'Other' becoming 70 (28 + 42). Here, however, the difference is not significant, so while we can say that there are significant factors involved relating to food type, we are unable to say that vegetables are completely predominant.

CUSTOMISING EXPECTED VALUES: CHI-SQUARE GOODNESS OF FIT

There are times when you will wish to compare your observed data with non-random expectations of data. Here is an obvious example from genetics.

Our hypothesis is that in a plot of self-fertilised pea plants, there will be a ratio of 3:1 for coloured flowers and white flowers. Gregor Mendel (1866) raised 929 of these, of which 705 had coloured flowers and 224 had white.

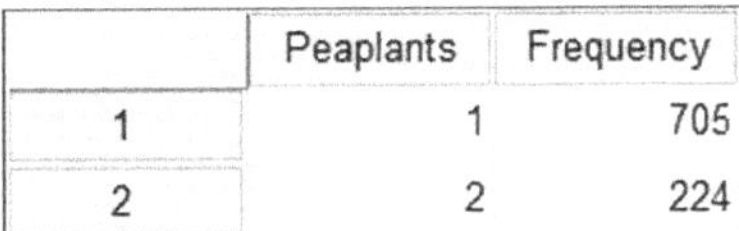

	Peaplants	Frequency
1	1	705
2	2	224

In this example, we use *Weight Cases* for the frequency variable, as we are using summary data. *Analyze/Nonparametric Tests/Legacy Dialogs/Chi-square.* Change the 'Expected Values' setting from 'All categories equal' to the 'Values' setting.

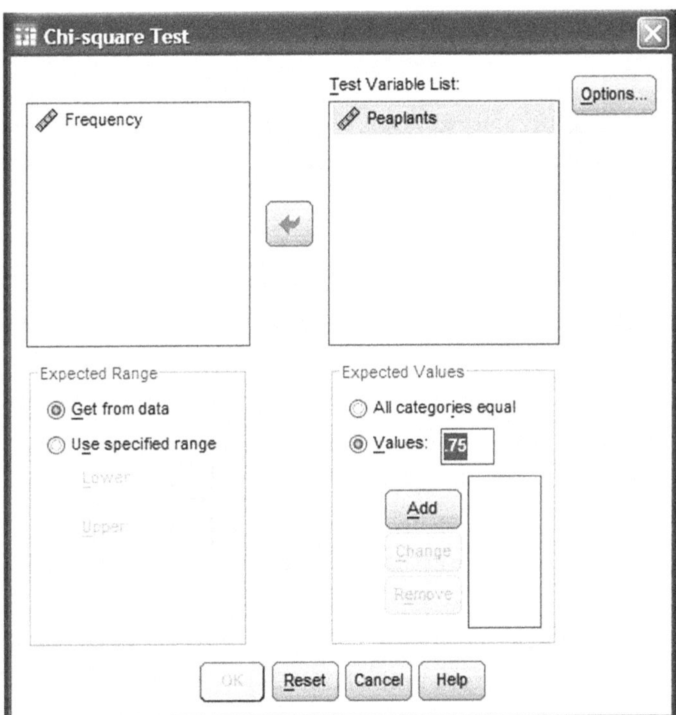

We then put in the proportion for the first value as a percentage of the total, then pressing 'Add' to transfer into the box on the bottom right. We continue with any further values, populating the box accordingly. Be careful to ensure that these are entered in the correct order.

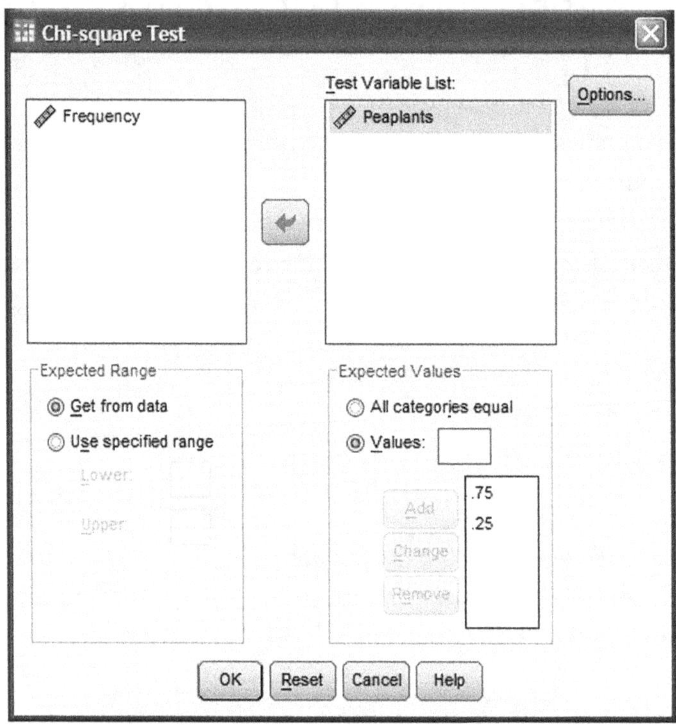

The Chi-square statistic is a tiny .391 and the very high significance level ($p > 0.5$) indicates that the null hypothesis is accepted. There is no evidence to suggest any deviation from the expected proportions.

This test can be used with more than two conditions. Mendel (1866) also found the following results from pea hybrids: round/yellow, 315; round/green, 108; wrinkled/yellow 101; and wrinkled/green 32. The expected ratio was 9:3:3:1 so we want to see if the findings were consistent.

The only essential difference from the last exercise is that we have four study variables as well as the frequency. The tricky bit is to make sure that the four percentages are entered appropriately in the 'Expected Values' section of Chi-square dialogue box.

So we work out the percentages. The ratios added together make 16. So we want (9/16) × 100 = 56.25%; (3/16) × 100 = 18.75%; another 3 gives 18.75% again; and (1/16) × 100 = 6.25%. So, in the box we will want to put: .5625; .1875; .1875; .0625.

If you entered the numbers correctly, you will find that the observed and expected values were very similar, with another tiny Chi-square and a super high significance value ($p > 0.9$). So we have a non-significant result, indicating that there is close agreement between the observations and the expected proportions.

RELATIONSHIPS BETWEEN VARIABLES: CHI-SQUARE TEST OF ASSOCIATION

This test examines the relationship between variables. As well as requiring nominal data and exclusivity, as mentioned previously, here we also need at least 20 observations in the sample, with at least 5 in each category.

If we wish to test the theory that blue-eyed people have better eyesight than other people, we could examine the relationship between eye colour and eyesight. The data (fictional, loosely adapted from Parker 1979) comprises the number of individuals in each combination of categories.

Table 7.3

Vision	Eye colour	
	Blue	**Other**
Normal	46	42
Short	23	17
Long	11	15

Data entry

In Variable View, create variables 'Colour', 'Vision' and 'Frequency'. Convert the Type for Colour and Vision to 'String' (for words), adjusting the width variables if you are going to enter long words). The only necessary change to Frequency is to adjust Decimal to zero.

Type the data into Data View. The spelling and case need to be identical throughout.

	Colour	Vision	Frequency
1	Blue	Normal	46
2	Blue	Short	23
3	Blue	Long	11
4	Other	Normal	42
5	Other	Short	17
6	Other	Long	15

Data/Weight Cases. Select *'Weight Cases by'*. Then transfer Frequency to the Frequency Variable box. Press 'OK'. (Ignore any SPSS warning about missing data when using summary data. Do not use the Weight Cases procedure if you are entering raw data.)

Analysis

Analyze/Descriptive Statistics/Crosstabs. In the Crosstabs dialog box, transfer the category with the most levels (here, Vision) to the Row(s) box and the one with less levels (Colour) to the Column(s). This avoids over-wide tables. Press the 'Statistics' button: select 'Chi-square' and 'Phi and Cramer's V'. After 'Continue', press 'Cells' and select 'Observed', 'Expected' and 'Round cell counts'. Press 'Continue', then 'OK' in the Crosstabs dialog box.

When viewing the output, it is generally worth checking the Case Processing Summary to make sure that you have the right number of cases. The table suggests no great dissimilarities between the observed and expected counts; this is supported by the high significance value of .481 which indicates a non-significant result.

Eyesight * Eye colour Crosstabulation

			Eye colour		
			Blue	Other	Total
Eyesight	Long	Count	11	15	26
		Expected Count	13.5	12.5	26.0
	Normal	Count	46	42	88
		Expected Count	45.7	42.3	88.0
	Short	Count	23	17	40
		Expected Count	20.8	19.2	40.0
Total		Count	80	74	154
		Expected Count	80.0	74.0	154.0

Let us look at another example. Again, we want to find out whether or not the interaction between variables is significant. Here, the relationship is between having seen a promotion and concern over an environmental issue. We use the same procedures as above to examine a 2 by 2 option.

Table 7.4

		Have you seen the promotion about this environmental issue?	
		Yes	**No**
Are you concerned with this issue?	**Yes**	18	12
	No	12	30

	Awareness	Concern	Frequency
1	Seen	Worried	18
2	Seen	Serene	12
3	Not seen	Worried	12
4	Not seen	Serene	30

Promotion seen * Concerned Crosstabulation

			Concerned		Total
			Serene	Worried	
Promotion seen	Not seen	Count	30	12	42
		Expected Count	24.5	17.5	42.0
	Seen	Count	12	18	30
		Expected Count	17.5	12.5	30.0
Total		Count	42	30	72
		Expected Count	42.0	30.0	72.0

The cross-tabulation table shows clear differences between the observed and expected results. The tests indicate that these differences are significant:

Chi-Square Tests

	Value	df	Asymp. Sig. (2-sided)	Exact Sig. (2-sided)	Exact Sig. (1-sided)
Pearson Chi-Square	7.112[a]	1	.008		
Continuity Correction[b]	5.878	1	.015		
Likelihood Ratio	7.168	1	.007		
Fisher's Exact Test				.015	.008
N of Valid Cases	72				

a. 0 cells (.0%) have expected count less than 5. The minimum expected count is 12.50.

b. Computed only for a 2x2 table

The top row is of interest here. The significance statistic is .008, $p < .01$ two-tailed. (Fisher's Exact test is for small data sets. Exactly how small is a matter for debate, but some authorities suggest this is where any cell has a frequency of 5 or less.)

As the result is significant, it is worth considering the effect size, using either Phi or Cramer's V, which we encounter in the 'Symmetric Measures' output. Here, both have a value of .314 with an approximate *p* value of .008.

Effect size for the Chi-square test of association

For 2 by 2 tables, as in this case, use Phi. With larger contingency tables, Cramer's V is preferred.

Opinion is divided on how to use these statistics. Some report the value (here, .314) as a correlation coefficient. I prefer to square Phi or Cramer's V, which provides an effect size reflecting its proportional influence on the variance. Here, we square the value of 0.314: $0.314 \times 0.314 = 0.0986$.

These categories of effect size are recommended (Kinnear and Gray 2004):

* Small: < 0.01 (under 1% of the variance)
* Medium: 0.01 to 0.10 (1 to 10% of the variance)
* Large: > 0.10 (over 10% of the variance).

Our figure of .0986 is almost 0.1.

The differences between observed and predicted values are clearly important – and the bigger the differences, the better – but the more classifications we have, the less meaningful our interpretations are likely to become. As with other statistical tests, you should select meaningful data rather than merely dredging.

DISCUSSION POINT

It may go against the grain to say so, but some figures are truly unquantifiable. Unreliable data will probably undermine any statistical analysis. Similarly, lack of a sensible 'starting point' or rationale may make quantification pointless.

However, there are times when people declare their precious subject to be unmeasurable. Their argument is usually from the perspective of personal preference rather than from any understanding of statistical methodology.

However, let me take their side for a while. An interview may offer insights into what lies behind wads of otherwise meaningless data. It may also be important to find out if the viewpoint of the interviewee is shared by others; this can of course be quantified.

The interview, or other qualitative data, can also be used as a starting point for thinking about new directions to investigate. Without a qualitative focus, how can we decide which of many potential experiments are worth conducting? Essentially, there should be a relationship between statistical analysis and interpretation. How far these should be kept separate is of course debatable.

This table refers to *frequencies of observations* within *categories* of a sample.

Table 7.5

Number of variables	Number of conditions	Focus	Test
One	2 (dichotomy)	differences	binomial test
One	2 (repeated dichotomy)	correlated differences	McNemar test
One	more than 2	differences	Chi-square goodness of fit
One	2 or more (non-random expectations)	similarities (non-significance shows consistency with expected ratios)	Chi-square goodness of fit (with adjusted expectedvalues)
Multi-variable	2 or more	interaction between variables	Chi-square test of association

CHAPTER 8

The time until events

The previous chapter involved *qualitative* data, information that is not measurable and can only be analysed in terms of one type of data differing from another. The qualities of any given category are its determining features.

I thought long and hard before deciding to make this a separate chapter. Again, each observation is not measurable in terms of size or weight. However, the analysis of the time until events does not look at differences in attributes; it looks instead at a single category of data occurring over time. Observations are not examined as categories but as a series of *events*.

What I call 'the time until events' is often referred to as *survival analysis*, because this set of techniques is commonly used in medicine, where the death of patients appears to be a popular cause for concern. However, this terminology ignores the wide range of possible applications for this type of statistical study, which is reflected in its history.

One of the oldest areas of statistics, it started with seventeenth century actuarial tables. Later, it was used in engineering to study how long it took for weapons to fail. This came to be known as reliability analysis or reliability theory.

Yet more names for the same set of techniques appear in different disciplines. I prefer 'time to event analysis', but other names turn up in areas of economics and sociology: duration analysis, duration modelling, event history analysis and event structure analysis. The different names probably account for the absence of this type of analysis from general statistical introductions by other authors.

Events can be both positive and negative. Medically, we could be interested in the length of time before an operation takes place; the event could be the point in time at which the patient is wheeled into the operating theatre (or the knife goes in, if you're feeling either more precise or a tad bloodthirsty). Studies of health and wellbeing often include life events such as births and deaths, graduating and dropping out, marriages and divorces, new jobs and lost jobs.

These techniques offer less predictive value than the measurement-oriented linear techniques found elsewhere in this book. On the other hand, they are much more versatile. Linearity is not a concern here (see the next chapter to see the dangers of not testing for linearity when using measurable data) and the techniques are amazingly adaptable to many real life problems. Perrigot *et al.* (2004) examine the history of failures within business franchises to study what works organisationally and what does not. You could also study car crashes or violent incidents.

As will be noted, it is also possible to contrast different categories. This could be the implementation of a new device in more than one type of setting, or its use against a 'control' setting where no such device is in place. Although care should be taken when comparing settings: Kahneman (2011) notes the dangers of epidemiological studies involving urban and rural settings, where large apparent differences can appear because of small data sets, with rural fluctuations resembling nothing so much as a few throws of the dice.

The time until events (or survival analysis, if you so wish) is concerned with how long it takes for an outcome, or **event**, to take place. The focus is on the interval between a given starting point and a specified event. A medical example could have the completion of a course of treatment as the starting point and the complete absence of symptoms as the event. The interval between the two points is referred to as the **survival time, observation period** or **follow-up period**.

The survival time is the area of examination. Do events tend to accelerate in frequency after a particular period of time? Are there phases in which events tend to cluster? What proportion of cases are affected in a particular phase?

We may also wish to contrast different samples. Does a group of workers under a special diet truly have a different accident rate from a control group on a traditional diet? Will the incidence of nuclear meltdowns differ according to the type of air conditioning at power stations?

There are other ways of measuring event rates, for example moving averages or using the predictive power of linear regression (see the next chapter). The analysis of the time until events, however, has a range of advantages. It is largely descriptive, providing a far more informative analysis of the process under investigation. Non-linear patterns are not a problem; we would not be concerned about measuring mortality studies, for example, where there will be inevitable shifts from the central tendency at the beginning and end of the follow-up period. Crucially, however, it also accounts for missing information, known as **censored events**.

Some information cannot be observed. This 'censored' information is often where the event in question fails to occur until after expiration of the follow-up period. The fact, for example, that a death or a promotion at work (to be more optimistic) does not happen within the survival time does not mean that such an event has not happened after the end of the study. Similarly, individuals who have withdrawn from medical studies or with whom researchers have lost contact (**loss to follow-up**), may or may not experience the medical event eventually. Even when we are certain that an event will take place (we are all dead in the long run, said Keynes), we cannot know *when*.

To merely omit censored data, or to count it as having the same duration as the latest recorded event, is to underestimate the effect under investigation. To focus on events in isolation would be to miss the considerable richness of data provided by looking at the time preceding them.

The time until events, also known as survival analysis, measures the occurrence of events in terms of the duration of time in which they take place. It also takes into account censored data. Information which is missing either during and after the monitoring period is called right censored data', which is easily accounted for. You should avoid introducing 'left censored data', where complications precede the survival time; there are procedures for dealing with some of this, but this cannot be covered in an introductory book.

STATISTICAL ASSUMPTIONS

Some assumptions about the data are required. Continuous data is needed for the follow-up time. In the case of the Kaplan–Meier survival function, this is usually days. Longer intervals such as years should be measured by life tables. Each record must be a different case; it must not be included more than once. Censoring should be random; do not exclude cases from the survival period because they appear to be a particularly high or low risk. The event should be categorical; cases are either dead or alive, cured or not, etc.

Methodologically speaking, the predictor variable is time and the criterion variable is the status. This is the opposite of the usual statistical situation.

THE KAPLAN–MEIER SURVIVAL FUNCTION

This requires the SPSS Advanced Module.

The beauty of the Kaplan–Meier is the intuitiveness of the survival plot. Its steepness shows the likelihood of an event, whether or not it accelerates or decelerates over time, and it can graphically demonstrate differences between groups of cases under different conditions.

Data entry

The minimum requirements are two variables. One is the follow-up time (or 'survival time'), a scale measure; this is usually days or hours. The other is either the event or the loss to follow-up of a case (a 'censored event'). I suggest using '1' for events and '0' for censored data. So each time represents either the event (death, absence of symptoms, etc.) or a withdrawal from the study.

Using a grouping variable is also quite a common occurrence, using the 'nominal' measure for the comparison of performances.

Analysis

EXERCISE 1

	Days	Rehoused
1	40	Rehoused
2	60	Rehoused
3	62	Rehoused
4	80	Rehoused
5	85	Rehoused
6	108	Rehoused
7	108	Rehoused
8	115	Censored
9	140	Rehoused
10	160	Censored
11	180	Censored
12	180	Censored

A new physiotherapy program has been completed by a group of hospitalised patients with severe mobility problems. The study lasts for 180 days. The target event for each patient is the achievement of independent living, according to pre-agreed criteria for successful adaptation. Censored data are patients dying, moving out of the area to other hospitals, etc.

We are using a small data set for the purpose of introducing this form of analysis.

In *Variable View*, 'Days' and 'Rehoused' are the variables to be created. Rehoused should be nominal, with the values of 0 for 'Censored' and 1 for 'Rehoused' (to turn the labels on or off, use *View/Value Labels*). The interval times are typed in *Data View* as above.

Analyze/Survival/Kaplan–Meier. Transfer 'Days' to the 'Time' field on the right. Transfer 'Rehoused' to the 'Status' field. Underneath the Status box, press '*Define Event*'. Leave it as 'Single value' and type in the number '1'. (Do not be concerned about the zero, as SPSS assumes this to be the censored event.) Press 'Continue'.

Having returned to the Kaplan–Meier dialog box, press 'Options'. Select 'survival tables', 'mean and median survival' and, from the plots submenu, 'survival' ('hazard' will appear in the next exercise). Press 'Continue', then in the main dialog box, 'OK'.

Now to the output. The initial summary data indicates correct data input (8 events, 4 censored). The survival table tells the story in numerical form:

The first successful rehabilitation takes place on the fortieth day. Subsequent rehousings take place until day 108, when two people move on the same day. Day 115 contains censored data; perhaps somebody moved to another catchment area. We then get another rehousing and another piece of censored data on day 160. The remaining two members of the cohort are not rehoused by the last day of observation, day 180, so they become censored data.

The survival table repeats the statistical input, but with two important additions: The number of cumulative events, omitting censored data, and the Estimate column, providing the proportion of the cohort still unaffected by events after a period of time (e.g. almost 92% after 40 days and about 31% after 140). This is initially calculated by dividing the number of unaffected cases by the total, but after the first censored event, the Kaplan–Meier adjusts the figure to an estimate to take into account any censored data.

Then comes the mean and median survival times. With larger data sets, the confidence intervals will become more important (as in the next exercise).

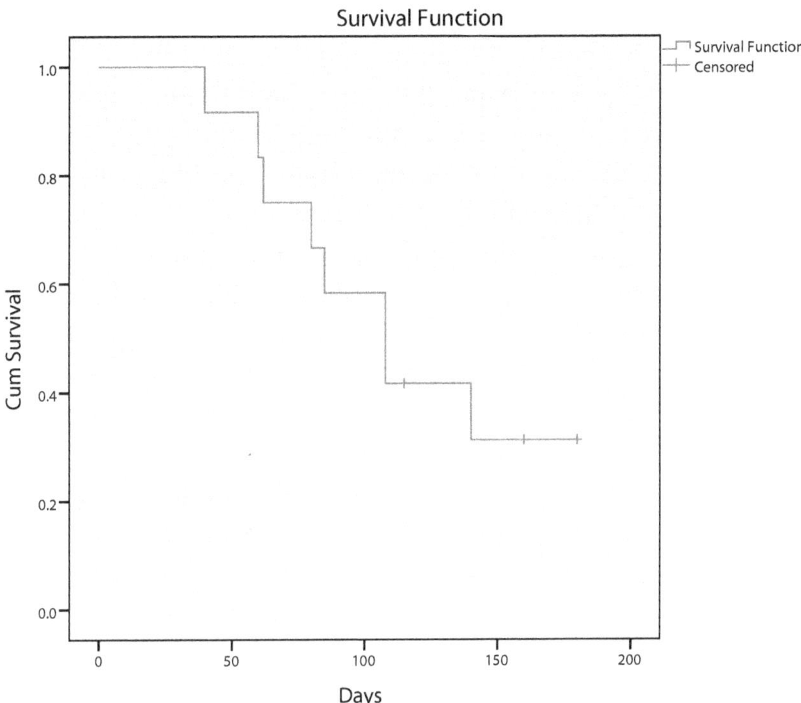

Events on the survival function chart are usually marked by a drop of the same depth, but a bigger drop can be seen on day 108, representing two events. Censored data are marked by a cross, but do not affect the shape of the survival function.

Kaplan–Meier takes into account censored data but makes no assumptions about the effect, the rate of rehousing. The calculations of the likelihood of an event have been worked out on the plot. The y axis, referred to as 'cumulative survival', runs from 0 to 1, from zero to 100% of the cases in the study. At 1, we have 100% of the cohort unaffected. After the first event, after 40 days, it looks like a little over 90% are unaffected. Returning to the survival table, you will see this as .917. If we call it 92%, then we can say that the probability of rehousing after 40 days is approximately 8% (100%–92%). (In real life, we would not make extrapolations so early with such a small sample.)

Then we look at the middle of the y axis and across to the intercept (where an imaginary horizontal line would meet the function line). The x axis value is the estimated median survival time, 108 days. Do note that the median is indeed an estimate; when seriously considering larger samples, the confidence intervals become very important.

The above procedure is all that is required, but you can also do a comparison with another group, as in the next exercise.

EXERCISE 2

Now we examine a more complicated sample. We are testing the reliability of a new mechanism for generating electricity from waves in the sea. There are two conditions: a batch of the new gadgets in a range of sea areas forms the experimental group, with the control group being existing mechanisms set up in the same areas.

The follow-up period is 90 days after installation of the two batches of generating equipment. In each case, we have measured days until the event. The event, a negative one this time, is the breakdown of the mechanism. The censored data comprises where the gadget has disappeared (this may be caused by vandalism, shipping collisions or the appearance of a kraken) or is otherwise 'lost to follow-up' (e.g. a coastguard has objected to the presence of one of the gadgets in a specific area). Or, the mechanism may still be working at the end of the observation period.

In Variable View, we need a 'days' variable, a status variable (value = 1 for breakdown and value = 0 for censored data) and a group variable (Experimental group = 1 and Control group = 2). The status and group variable Measures should be set to 'Nominal'. Set 'Decimals' to zero.

In Data View, type in the data below in the following way: the number goes in the days column. The default in the status variable is 1, except where I have placed a zero in parentheses, representing censored data. The grouping variable column should hold 1 for the experimental group and 2 for the control group.

Experimental group (15 cases):

* 27, 29 (0), 40, 54, 60, 72, 83, 84, 88, 90 (0), 90 (0), 90 (0), 90 (0), 90 (0), 90 (0).

Control group (15 cases):

* 16, 17, 18, 20, 22, 25, 25, 30 (0), 53, 71, 84, 86, 90 (0), 90 (0), 90 (0).

At the moment, we will analyse the whole sample, so do not use the grouping variable. Run the procedure as you did in the previous exercise, but within the Options dialog, add the Hazard plot to the previous selections.

Part of the output comprises a very large survival table. The data presents the following narrative: breakdowns start to occur in the control group after the first two weeks following installation. By the end of the month, one experimental mechanism has broken down and another has been lost to follow-up for whatever reason. As the weeks go by, some more breakdowns occur in both groups. By the end of the 90 day period, 6 mechanisms from the experimental batch survive the observation period without breakdown (note that the Kaplan–Meier, during the calculations, does not ignore the possibility of a future breakdown). Three of the control group mechanisms also survive the follow-up period without breaking down.

Do note the number of censored events at the end of the row of figures. A high number may mean that many cases fail to experience the event in question; but a more plausible explanation is that the follow-up period does not last long enough to take into account enough observations. We can say here, however, that there is a 51% survival likelihood after 72 days (49% are likely to break down by then).

On the other hand, 33% are likely to continue working up to or beyond 90 days.

The table is followed by the means and medians. While the mean survival time is 64 days, the confidence intervals indicate that values will typically fall between about 54 and 74 days. Citing confidence intervals can be rather useful for predicting. Do note that in reports we generally cite the median survival time, here 83 days with confidence intervals of about 66 and 99 days.

The role of the confidence intervals should become clearer when you examine the survival function. Looking at the mean's confidence intervals first, you will see that an awful lot happens in the period between 54 and 74 days. The median as a statistic of central tendency shows something different, the central values; the confidence intervals portray a considerable flurry of activity between 66 and 99 days. The median is generally considered to be more useful than the mean in survival analysis and as shown, the confidence intervals are highly informative.

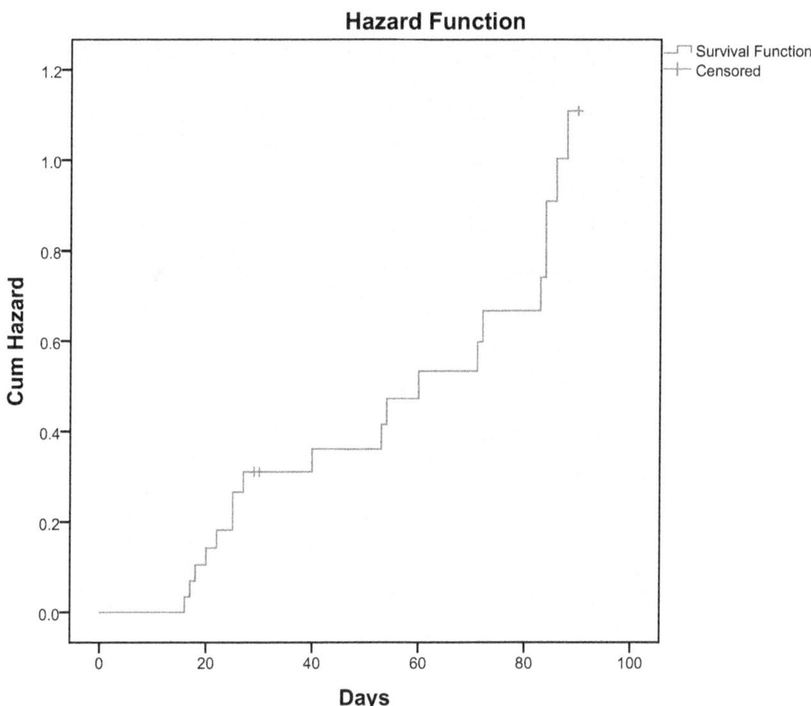

The hazard plot denotes the relative acceleration of risk, the y axis representing 'cumulative hazard'. It indicates a steep trend of breakdowns in the third week, with a rather pronounced trend towards the end of the follow-up period.

Please save your data.

EXERCISE 3

Using the same sample as in the previous exercise, we will contrast the two groups. *Analyze/Survival/Kaplan–Meier*. This time, transfer the grouping variable to the 'Factor' slot. (You would use 'Strata' if there were different conditions to contrast, e.g. with and without monthly servicing, which would need another variable). Also, press 'Compare Factor', selecting all three test statistics: Log Rank, Breslow and Tarone–Ware.

The survival table appears in two sub-divisions, one per group. We can see at the bottom of each division the number of mechanisms that have lasted up to or beyond the 90 day observation period: 6 in the experimental group and 3 in the control group. There are also clear differences between the groups in the rest of the survival data. Little more than 50% of the control group are likely to carry on working after 30 days, while in the same period there is very little movement within the experimental group. By the end of follow-up, only 23% of the controls are likely to carry on working (77% breakdown likelihood), compared to 43% of the experimental group. The means and medians tell a similar story (note that the median survival time is generally considered more useful in survival analysis than the mean), although the confidence intervals are somewhat less informative with these smaller sub-samples.

Tests of significance in the time until events

Before seeing if the differences in our example are significantly different, we must consider the tests of significance offered by SPSS.

The Log Rank test is best when testing a survival curve through its entire course and is more sensitive when the two groups show consistently similar patterns.

The Breslow test is considered more sensitive to differences between groups in the early stages. This test can, however, tend towards Type Two errors (judging results not to be significant when they are, a 'False Negative'. The opposite, by the way, is a Type 1 error, a 'False Positive', seeing significance when it should be absent).

The Tarone–Ware test is preferred where survival curves intersect or move away from each other.

When we look at the survival functions and consider the descriptions above, the Breslow is the most appropriate test for this data set. It indicates significant differences between the groups, p value = .029, critical value $p < .05$.

(If we look just out of interest at the less appropriate tests, the differences appear, unsurprisingly, to be insignificant under the Log Rank test (.083), reflecting the differences between the two groups' patterns. Tarone–Ware, however, shows $p < .05$ which hints at the dangers of dredging.)

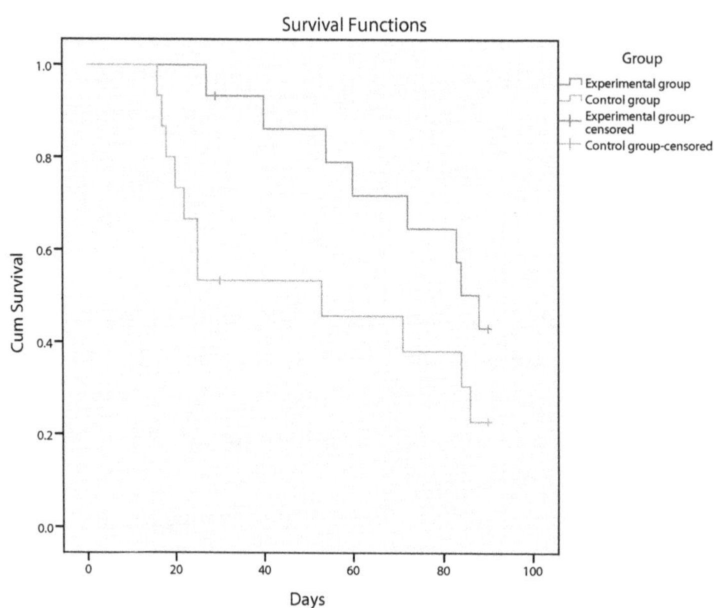

The survival plot tells an interesting story. The control group, on the lower line, start to break down very quickly, within about a week. If this is usual technically, then fine, it shows that the new mechanism would appear not to break down over this period. It would be worth checking, however, in case something unusual affected some of these mechanisms at this time. There would appear to be a clear difference between the groups over time, but with a similar decline towards the end, which does suggest that the observation time should have been longer.

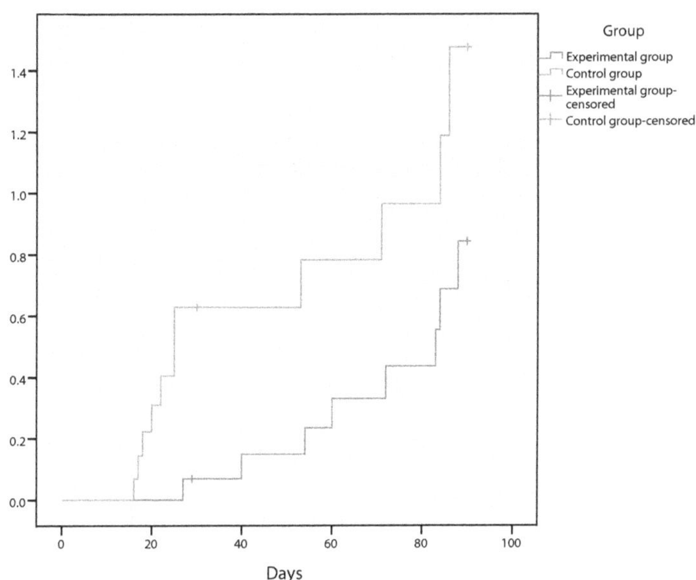

The hazard plot shows a clear increase in risk among the control group in the early period. Increased risk appears at the end for both groups. At the very least, we should be concerned about the possible vulnerability of all mechanisms during the third month. (Reminder: this was a fictional study.)

Please keep this file for the next exercise.

THE LIFE TABLE

This requires the SPSS Advanced Module.

Generally speaking, you should use the Kaplan–Meier where possible, as it provides richer data. However, although it is a non-parametric instrument, the Kaplan–Meier is designed to analyse continuous data. If you want to study intervals as long as months, quarters and years, then a life table should be used. As with the Kaplan–Meier, the risk is adjusted to take account of losses to follow-up. The minimum sample size for a life table, in terms of the number of cases at the beginning of the study, should be at least 30, although some authorities recommend at least 100. Life tables typically analyse samples of thousands.

Frequently used in population ecology, one example of the use of life tables is in the analysis of a primate population (Assembly of Life Sciences 1981). We could analyse the population by recording deaths in different age classes (death-based), as with much of survival analysis in medicine, but primate census data tends towards observations of live primates (life-based).

However, to save space, we will use the data from the previous exercise on Kaplan–Meier. We now use a different part of the Survival Analysis submenu.

Analyze/Survival/Life Tables

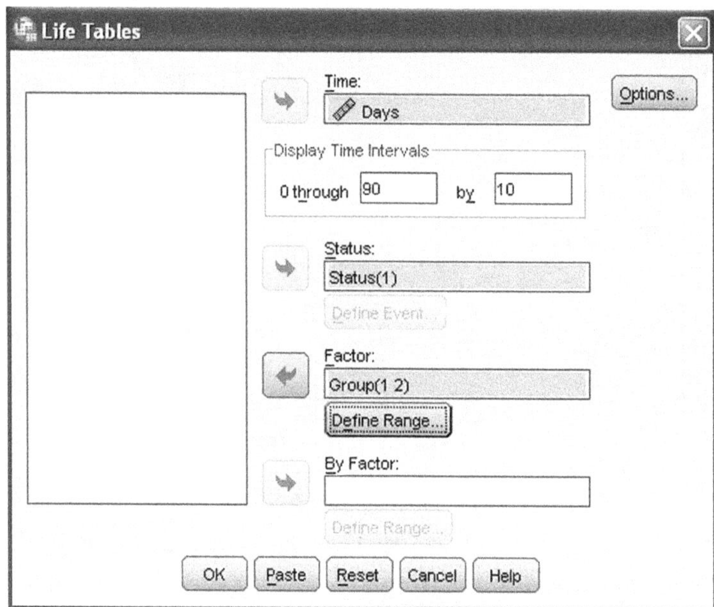

We transfer the Days variable to 'Time'. Both of the 'Display Time Intervals' slots must be completed. The first slot covers the data from 0 to 90 days. The second provides a fairly compact analysis by analysing the data in 10 day chunks. We then enter the Status variable into its slot; in 'Define Event' choose the single value option and enter 1 to represent the event.

Although the Factor slot is used here to show how it looks, I would not usually look at group variables in life tables with such a small sample.

However, in this example, we transfer the Group variable to the factor slot and in 'Define Range' enter '1' and '2' to represent the two groups.

The results are very similar to the Kaplan–Meier, but lack features such as the statistical tests of group differences and confidence intervals.

This table of survival analysis techniques only refers to tests used in this chapter:

Table 8.1

N.B. *Non-parametric tests can be used with 'parametric' data.*

Test	Data	Purpose
Kaplan–Meier	Non-parametric. Large and small sample. Data must be continuous (i.e. not less frequent than days).	Tracking events over time.
Life Table	Non-parametric. Large samples. Interval data (e.g. months, quarters, years).	Tracking events over time.
Log Rank Breslow Tarone–Ware	Non-parametric. For differences in usage, see earlier notes in this chapter.	Significance of Kaplan–Meier group differences.

SPSS also offers Cox's regression under the category 'survival analysis'. Also known as the Cox model, this provides a type of multiple regression technique (see the next chapter), allowing the weighting of different independent variables. The Cox is semi-parametric, requiring certain assumptions to be met about the data and is not suitable for an introductory text (and the same can be said for logit and probit).

DISCUSSION POINT

As mentioned earlier, we do not necessarily have to discuss life and death as events of interest; events can be positive or negative and not necessarily dramatic. Another point about this set of methods is that it stimulates research. As you pore over the tyre tracks of time, new questions arise. This type of statistical analysis asks 'a series of questions about the causal connections among actions ... It relentlessly probes the analyst's construction, comprehension and interpretation of the event.' (Griffin 2007).

CHAPTER 9

Correlations, regression and factor analysis

CORRELATION

Returning to data with measurable differences, we may wish to examine the relationship between one variable and another, its **correlation**. This is generally represented by the **correlation coefficient**, a statistic with the boundaries of +1 (a perfect positive correlation) and –1 (a perfectly negative relationship). If a result is near the mid-point, 0, then the results are likely to be random; there would be no ascertainable relationship between the variables.

This will be illustrated by the following numbers and the related scatter plots:

Table 9.1

1 2 3 4 5	1 2 3 4 5	These two columns are exactly the same, for example five questions in an opinion poll being answered in the same way by two different people. A graphical representation can be made with a spreadsheet scatter plot using Microsoft Excel or the OpenOffice Calc Chart Wizard, or using SPSS Graphs.

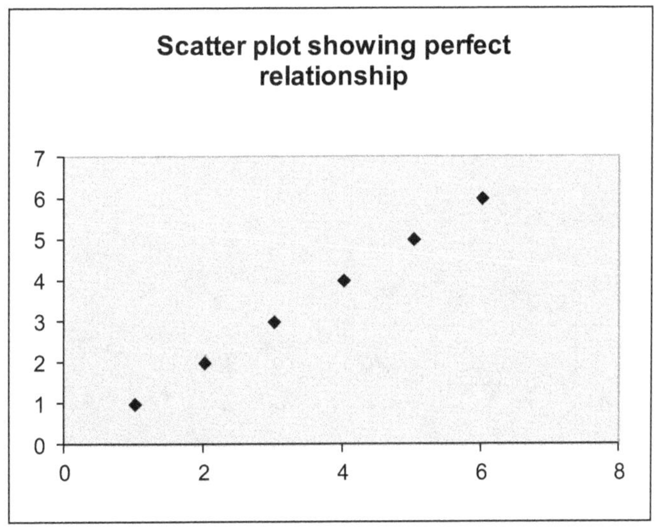

The above data subsets form a perfect positive correlation; a statistical test would produce a correlation coefficient of 1. A perfect relationship would be unlikely to appear in the course of research, but a similar slope indicates a positive relationship between two variables.

Table 9.2		
1 2 3 4 5	5 4 3 2 1	This is the inverse, a perfect negative relationship; the higher the score on one measure, the lower the score on the other.

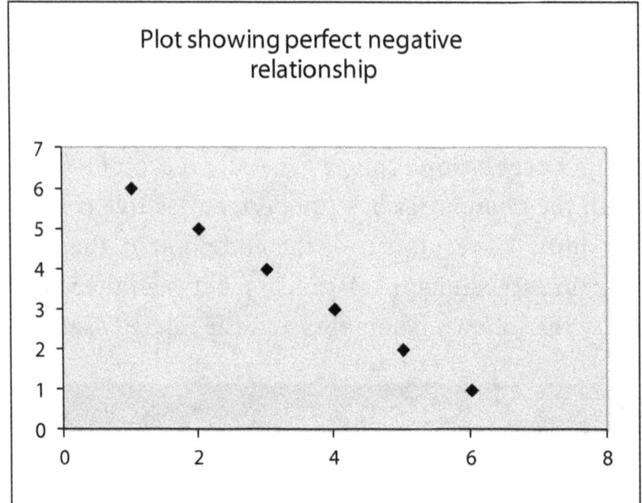

On this occasion, the slope rises from right to left, indicating a negative relationship. Statistically, a perfect negative correlation would be represented by a correlation coefficient of –1.

The next data set was randomly generated. No sensible slope is imaginable for this relationship. With a larger data set, a globular cluster would be typical.

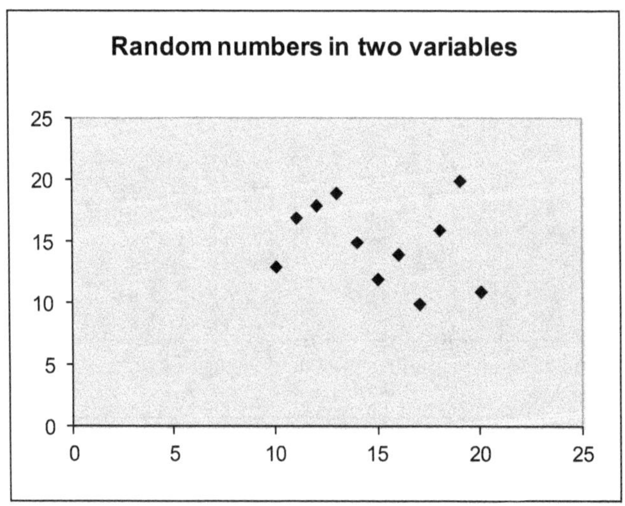

If you wish to reproduce this chart, use the following data:

Table 9.3

80	83
10	70
84	79
42	98
13	62
76	12
28	29
97	87
12	62
98	44

A random relationship will have a small correlation coefficient and a high significance value.

Effect sizes for correlations

The correlation coefficient is usually reported as *r*. If the test does not report an effect size, then it is simple to calculate merely by multiplying *r* by itself to get **r squared** (r^2). So, if *r* is 0.4, then *r* squared is 0.16. (Negative correlations turn positive when squared, so $r = -0.4$ also has the effect size of 0.16. Some calculators can't multiply negative values, so just multiply the equivalent positive values, such as 0.4 and 0.4, to get the effect size.)

Some people make the mistake of thinking that the '*p* value' is a measurement of the strength of the relationship; it is, in fact, a measure of significance, whether or not an effect exists as opposed to being an irrelevant comparison. Although the correlation coefficient *r* may be a useful as a rough guide to the relative effect size, r^2 is the effect size itself, measuring how far the effect accounts for the **variance**.

These effect size definitions are recommended for correlations (Kinnear and Gray 2004):

* Small: < 0.01 (under 1% of the variance)
* Medium: 0.01 to 0.10 (1 to 10%)
* Large: > 0.10 (over 10% of the variance).

Comparing two conditions, parametric version: Pearson

First, let us see what happens if we examine the simple data sets we have already looked at, representing a perfect positive relationship, a perfect negative one and the pair of variables with random scores.

DATA ENTRY

In Variable View, we want variable names for each of the paired conditions. 'Decimals' should be set to zero; the zero value can be copied from one cell to the others.

	Name	Type	Width	Decimals	Label	Values
1	Positive1	Numeric	8	0	Perfect positive A	None
2	Positive2	Numeric	8	0	Perfect positive B	None
3	Negative1	Numeric	8	0	Perfect negativ...	None
4	Negative2	Numeric	8	0	Perfect negativ...	None
5	Random1	Numeric	8	0	Random A	None
6	Random2	Numeric	8	0	Random B	None

In Data View, you should type in the following:

	Positive1	Positive2	Negative1	Negative2	Random1	Random2
1	1	1	1	6	80	83
2	2	2	2	5	10	70
3	3	3	3	4	84	79
4	4	4	4	3	42	98
5	5	5	5	2	13	62
6	6	6	6	1	76	12
7	.	.	.	.	28	29
8	.	.	.	.	97	87
9	.	.	.	.	12	62
10	.	.	.	.	98	44

You could save time by ignoring the variable creation stage, as Variable View would automatically create provisional variable names. Avoid making a habit of this, however, as this can lead to damaging errors in any but the simplest of exercises.

ANALYSIS

Analyze/Correlate/Bivariate. We use the default option, the Pearson test. Transfer the first two variables of interest into the right-hand box. Click 'OK'. (We could transfer all of the conditions into the box at one go, but let us avoid possible complications in the output.) The read-out gives the expected 1 for a perfect positive. The negative pairing gives –1. In both cases, we get a very low significance value.

There is a continuum of correlation coefficients:

Table 9.4

1 (perfect positive)	----------------------	**0** (perfectly random)	----------------------	**–1** (perfect negative)

Then look at the read-out for the randomised variables:

The Pearson correlation coefficient is .035, very close to zero. The significance value of .923 is very high, a very long way from the $p < .05$ or lower that we usually seek.

A FURTHER EXERCISE

Create a new file with two variables in Variable View, say 'TestA' and 'TestB'. These are diagnostic tests which may be used in future at different times (we may wish to avoid experiential effects such as patients remembering the questions). However, at the moment, we want to test their **reliability**, their consistency as measures. So the same people will take both tests to see if they do in fact produce comparable results. Type in the following data sets in Data View as parallel columns:

* 62, 56, 40, 37, 62, 56, 68, 55, 68, 60
* 65, 55, 39, 43, 66, 54, 73, 58, 72, 64.

Save this file as 'Parallels', to be used again later.

A scatter plot to examine the relationship between the two variables shows a clear positive slope. (I have used graphics from a spreadsheet, which are easier to modify than those of statistics packages.)

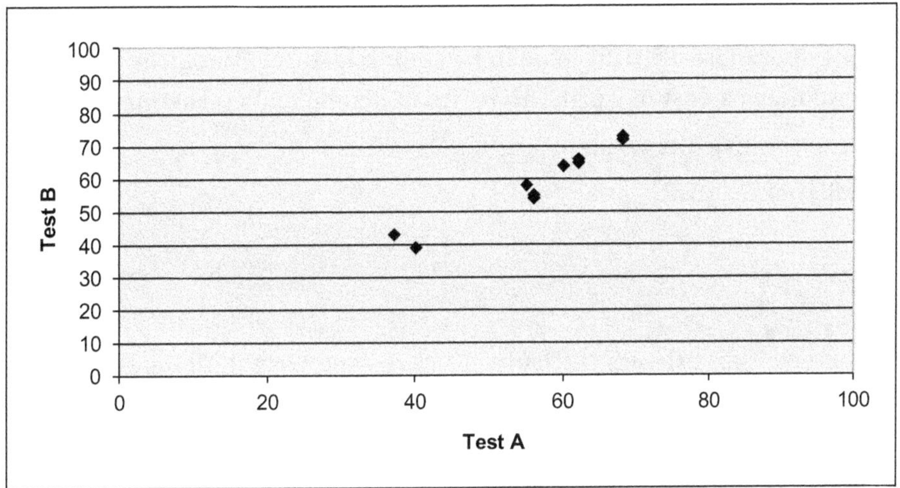

The Pearson is a parametric test, so we need to check for normal distribution. *Analyze/Descriptive Statistics/Explore*. Transfer both variables to the Dependent List box (they are both 'Scale' measures). Then press the 'Plots' button to select 'Normality plots with tests'.

The Shapiro–Wilk test is non-significant, so we are not concerned about non-normal data (Kolmogorov–Smirnov should be used with 50 or more cases). If the data proves to be unsuitable, use a non-parametric equivalent test, the Spearman or Kendall's tau-b.

The read-out gives similar means for both variables (56.4 and 58.9), each with a similar range (the difference between the minimum and the maximum figures). This suggests but does not prove a relationship between the two sets of data.

To create a more manageable read-out, use *Analyze/Descriptive Statistics/Descriptives*.

Analyze/Correlate/Bivariate. We use the Pearson test option with parametric data. Let us say that we have been uncertain as to whether or not the results would be close: use the two-tailed option. Transfer both variables. Select 'Options' and select 'Means and standard deviations' (which are generally used in reports). Then press 'Continue' and 'OK'.

The correlation coefficient is .971, highly significant: $p < .0005$ – it is highly unlikely to be a fluke result. The tests are clearly very reliable as parallels. Square the correlation of .971 to get the effect size. At 0.943, r^2 represents almost 95% of the variance; in other words, only just over 5% of the variance from the mean is likely to be caused by extraneous factors.

For an example of a non-significant result using Pearson's correlation, try comparing the following two variables:

* 52, 53, 47, 40, 48, 45, 52, 47, 51, 38
* 60, 34, 38, 52, 54, 55, 36, 48, 44, 56.

Comparing two conditions, non-parametric version: Spearman or Kendall's tau-b

As discussed previously, a non-parametric test is less choosy about the nature of the data. Here, we consider the potential for competing factors within engineering design. In the example of making an aircraft door more difficult to open by adding features, McCarthy (2009) considers it likely that there would be a cost in weight. Here, we use completely made-up data.

* ITEM 1: perceived difficulty rating
* ITEM 2: number of features.

DATA ENTRY

In Variable View, create the variables Difficulty, Features and Weight. In Data View, in the Difficulty column, enter the figures 1, 5, 4, 2, 2, 3, 1, 1, 3, 2 (this is a perceived difficulty rating). Under Features, enter the following: 5, 4, 5, 3, 1, 2, 4, 3, 2, 2 (here, we have the number of features added to create difficulty).

ANALYSIS

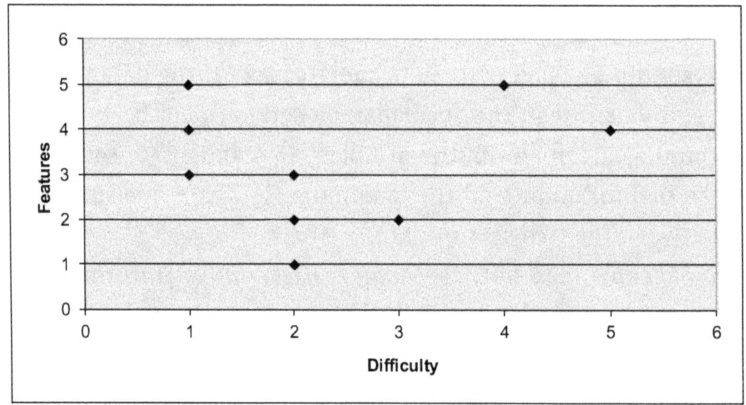

Having seen a fairly bitty scatter plot chart, we now use our non-parametric tests. *Analyze/Correlate/Bivariate*. Deselect the default Pearson option (for parametric data) and select Spearman, Kendall's tau-b or both. The two tests give slightly different results; Spearman is most frequently used, but some statisticians favour Kendall (e.g. Arndt *et al.* 1999).

We will assume uncertainty about whether or not the results would be close and use the two-tailed option.

The Spearman test coefficient turns out to be about –.06, obviously small. The significance level of 0.875 is very big, any effect being purely chance. The Kendall readings are similar, at close to –.08 and .776.

Now compare the 'Features' figures (the second set) with the following weights for each door: 280, 300, 250, 270, 180, 200, 150, 240, 180, 220.

ndom1	Random2	Difficulty	Features	Weight
80	83	1	5	280
10	70	5	4	300
84	79	4	5	250
42	98	2	3	270
13	62	2	1	180
76	12	3	2	200
28	29	1	4	150
97	87	1	3	240
12	62	3	2	180
98	44	2	2	220

Let us assume that the researcher had predicted beforehand that weight would be positively associated with the number of features. After selecting *Analyze/Correlate/Bivariate*, transfer the Features and Weight variables into the right-hand box and select 'one-tailed'. Given the small numbers, $p < .05$ was an acceptable level (5 in 100 chance of a fluke finding) and we may argue that theoretical likelihood means that the less rigorous one-tailed level of analysis is acceptable.

Correlations

			Number of features	Weight of doors
Kendall's tau_b	Number of features	Correlation Coefficient	1.000	.483*
		Sig. (1-tailed)	.	.032
		N	10	10
	Weight of doors	Correlation Coefficient	.483*	1.000
		Sig. (1-tailed)	.032	.
		N	10	10
Spearman's rho	Number of features	Correlation Coefficient	1.000	.572*
		Sig. (1-tailed)	.	.042
		N	10	10
	Weight of doors	Correlation Coefficient	.572*	1.000
		Sig. (1-tailed)	.042	.
		N	10	10

*. Correlation is significant at the 0.05 level (1-tailed).

We can reject the null hypothesis at $p < .05$ one-tailed. The two-tailed variation, with the significance values doubling, would not have been deemed significant (although in reality this would probably be because of the small sample).

So we have the worst of all worlds here. The number of features does not appear to relate to the difficulty of opening but it does have a bearing on the weight.

A scatter graph showing the relationship between the number of features and the weight of the doors shows a mild slope.

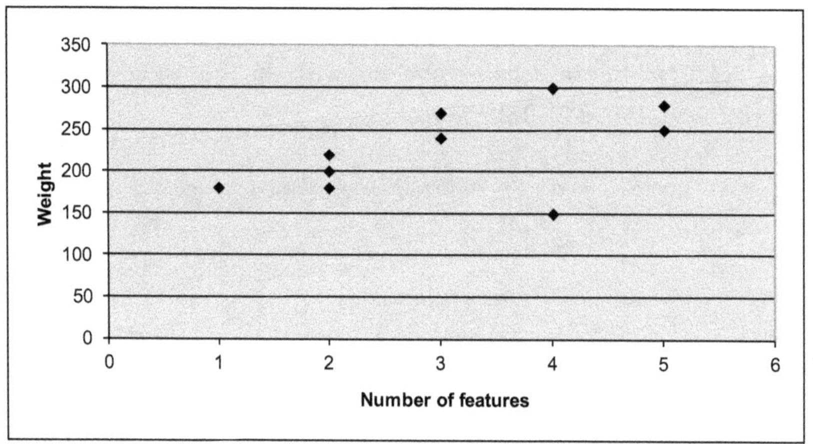

A cautionary note: You may have noticed my use of scatter plots in addition to test usage. This is because tests of correlation (non-parametric and parametric) are *linear*, assuming a relationship running in one direction, whether positive or negative. If you run a test without looking at a scatter plot as well, there is the danger of assuming significance or lack of it from completely misleading test results. Below are two examples of non-linear correlations.

The first is a real-life error. Blood pressure readings were measured against time. The coefficient was –0.16, with a two-tailed p value of .3 – this non-significant result was surprising as both the patient and the researcher had expected a pattern to emerge. Then, a scatter plot revealed the problem:

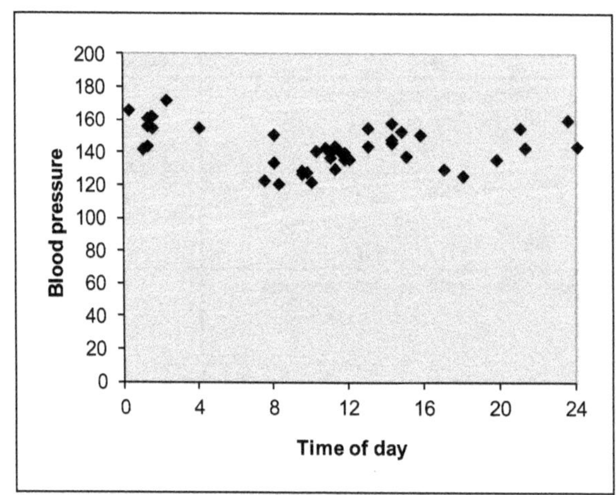

The graph's wave-like formation shows higher blood pressure readings in the early afternoon and at night. So there is an effect, but not a linear one. While the graph was informative, a linear test should not have been used with this data set. The correlations were of course meaningless. (What could have been done was to compare readings at the same time of day.)

Another non-linear example may be familiar to students of stress and to sports fans.

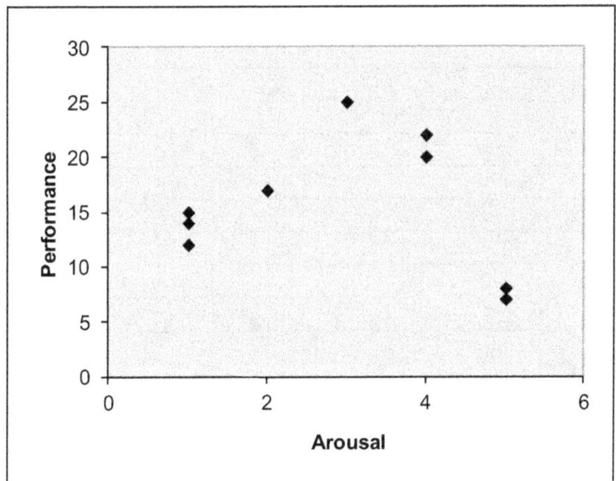

Fictional data is used here to illustrate the grading of sporting performance when subjected to high and low stress levels. The chart shows what is known as the Yerkes–Dodson Law (Yerkes and Dodson 1908). Although high stress may damage performance, some degree of stimulation seems necessary. Again, this non-linear effect would emerge from a graph, but any results from a correlational test would be erroneous. Essentially, 'curvilinear' relationships should not be subjected to these tests. Once again, I wish to emphasise: data should be examined graphically before considering the use of tests.

REGRESSION

Near the end of our discussion of the Pearson test, we saw a correlation coefficient of .971, meaning a large effect size, 0.943. What if we had a more modest effect, such as a coefficient (r) of .55, the effect size ($r \times r$) being 0.3025, just 30% of the variance? Various questions emerge. If the rest of the variance is random 'noise', could the research model be improved, made more reliable? Is another factor at play which might contribute to our understanding of the effect? Is the significant result meaningful in real-world terms, and should we invest in it? These questions can be tackled in a practical way with multiple regression.

As a building block, however, we first need to consider regression as a concept.

Simple linear regression (two conditions)

The scatter plot for significant relationships between two diagnostic tests portrays a slope, representing the relationship. A trend line has been drawn through the incline. This could even be extended, taking us into the realms of prediction.

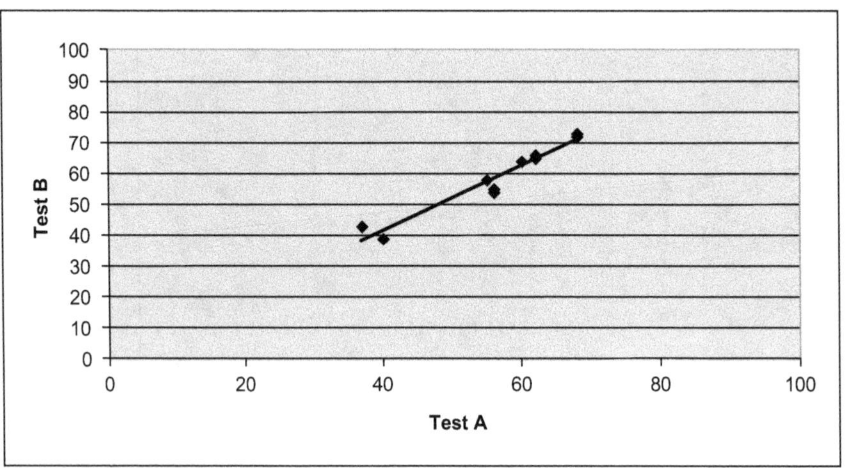

By looking at where the X variable meets the intercept (the line), we can see what value is expected from the Y variable. However, as real life often defies simple predictions, regression is more often used for creating models of what is likely to work in theory, with the intention of building better models.

Regression in SPSS is for parametric data. (A test for more rough-hewn data can be found in another statistics package, the inexpensive StatsDirect, where you would use *Analysis/Regression & Correlation/Non-Parametric Linear Regression*). However, as in the exercise below, ratings can usually be dealt with using SPSS, especially if the data is within reasonably normal bounds.

Let us consider a (fictional) study of dehydration in long distance runners. A rating scale represents how dried-up the runners are at a set point. Another rating scale measures how much they think they need a drink for rehydration. Dehydration (the predictor) is likely to determine the runners' awareness of needing a drink (the criterion).

DATA ENTRY

Data is entered as it was for correlations. In Variable View, enter 'Dehydration' and 'Awareness'.

In Data View, type in the following for 'Dehydration': 1, 1, 1, 2, 2, 2, 3, 3, 3, 4, 4, 4, 5, 5, 5 (the higher, the dryer) and for 'Awareness', the rated likelihood of their wanting a drink (the higher, the thirstier): 3, 1, 1, 2, 1, 2, 3, 2, 3, 2, 3, 4, 4, 5, 5.

ANALYSIS

Check for normal distribution using the Shapiro–Wilk test (Kolmogorov–Smirnov for 50 or cases). *Analyze/Descriptive Statistics/Explore*. Use the 'Plots' button to select 'Normality plots with tests'. Transfer both variables to the 'Dependent List'. The data in this exercise gives us no reason to assume non-normality so we can proceed. (From the *Explore* output, the means and standard deviation statistics are usually reported.)

Our interest is in how far the level of dehydration is likely to lead to awareness of dehydration. So dehydration is the predictor (in SPSS, independent variable) and awareness of dehydration, as manifested in a desire to drink, is the outcome (or criterion or dependent variable). In everyday terms, will dehydration be responded to safely by athletes independently judging their own bodily conditions?

Analyze/Regression/Linear. Transfer 'Dehydration', the predictor, to the Independent(s) box and 'Awareness', the criterion, to the Dependent box.

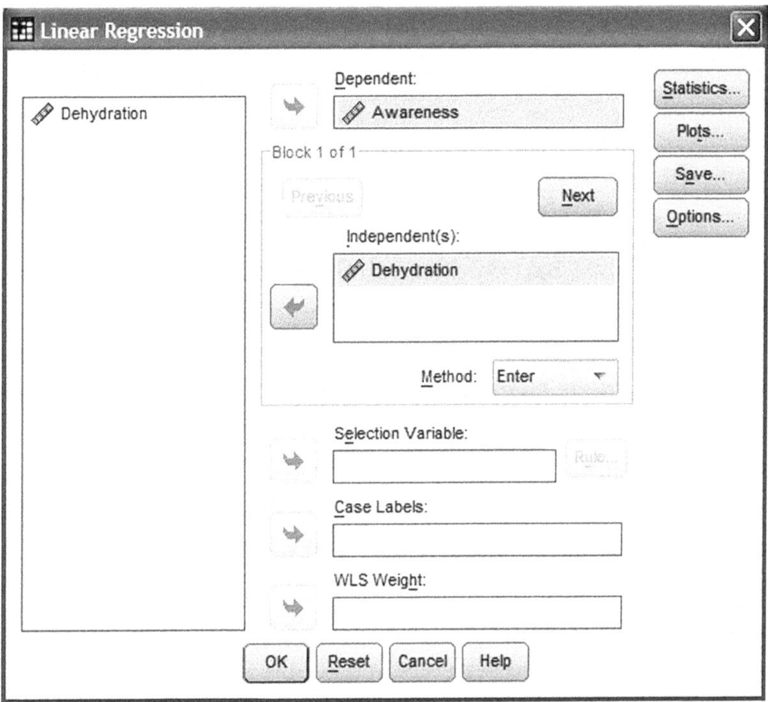

Image 9.14

Press 'OK'. The output *p* value will be .000 with the highly significant critical value of $p < .0005$ The standardised coefficient is a very large .804.

With regression, we do not need to square the coefficient to get the effect size, as SPSS provides this in the 'Model Summary'. *R Square* = .647, but generally we accept the slightly more modest *Adjusted R Square* (.620), which is still very large.

Effect sizes for regression

* Small: < .01 (less than 1% of the variance)
* Medium: 0.01 – 0.10 (1 to 10% of the variance)
* Large: > 0.10 (more than 10% of the variance).

Now create a scatter plot using a spreadsheet chart. The scatter plot is the only way to be sure of a truly linear relationship between the two variables.

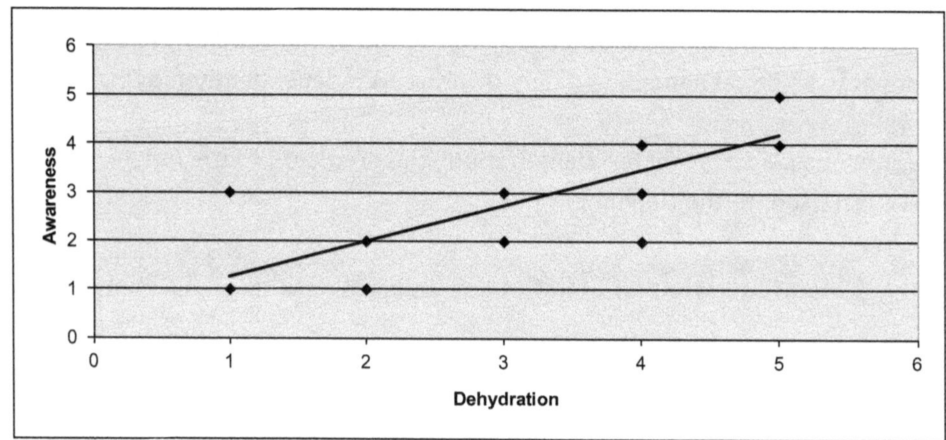

Looking at the intercept, from 'Chart/Add Trendline' on another package, it seems possible (with more data, we would have more confidence) that athletes with higher levels of dehydration are more likely to want a drink, while this may be somewhat less likely at an intermediate level. Perhaps those with an intermediate level of dehydration are insufficiently aware of potential problems.

The commercial data set below, analysing (fictional) sales of wool, provides a more detailed example of regression. For the moment, we will look only at Sales and Price. Is there a meaningful relationship between them, and can we predict how well wool will sell if we change the price? (Before anybody blames me for going bust, these are fictional figures. 'Pile High, Sell Cheap' works in some markets and not in others ...)

In Variable View, type in Farm, Sales, Price, Online, Radio and Press, perhaps with the labels 'Farm number', 'Sales numbers', 'Average price', 'Online marketing', 'Local radio' and 'Local press'. Adjust Decimal to zero for most variables, but leave 'Price' with 2 decimal places. Then type the numbers in Data View as below and save the file, perhaps as 'sales'; the additional data will be used for multiple regression shortly.

Table 9.5					
Farm	**Sales**	**Price**	**Online**	**Local radio**	**Local press**
1	8600	24.99	2180	6400	12 000
2	9100	18.99	2200	7800	11 500
3	9400	24.99	2220	6800	12 400
4	9500	24.99	2160	7000	13 500
5	9800	18.99	2220	6500	13 200
6	10 700	18.99	2170	5000	13 500
7	11 200	18.99	2280	6800	13 200
8	11 400	18.99	2500	7200	13 500
9	11 400	18.99	2200	6000	13 500
10	11 700	18.99	2250	7400	12 900
11	3800	30.99	2190	5000	11 000
12	4900	30.99	2250	7500	12 000
13	6100	24.99	1180	5400	11 900
14	6500	30.99	2250	6000	12 500
15	6900	30.99	2170	8200	12 100
16	7300	30.99	2180	6500	14 000
17	7400	20.99	2255	6100	12 200
18	7600	30.99	2250	6800	12 300
19	7800	18.99	2200	6000	13 300
20	8100	20.99	2240	6900	10 000
21	11 800	30.99			

(For the sake of the exercise, limited data has been used, not all of it from a normal distribution.)

Analyze/Regression/Linear. Transfer 'Sales' to the Dependent box and 'Price' to the Independent box, ensure that the method box reads 'enter'. Press 'OK'.

The Correlation Coefficient reads –0.605, the negative representing an inverse relationship: lower prices, higher sales, $p < .01$. The effect size, *Adjusted R Square*, is .333, so the relationship between the two variables only accounts for a third of the variance. The implications will be discussed shortly.

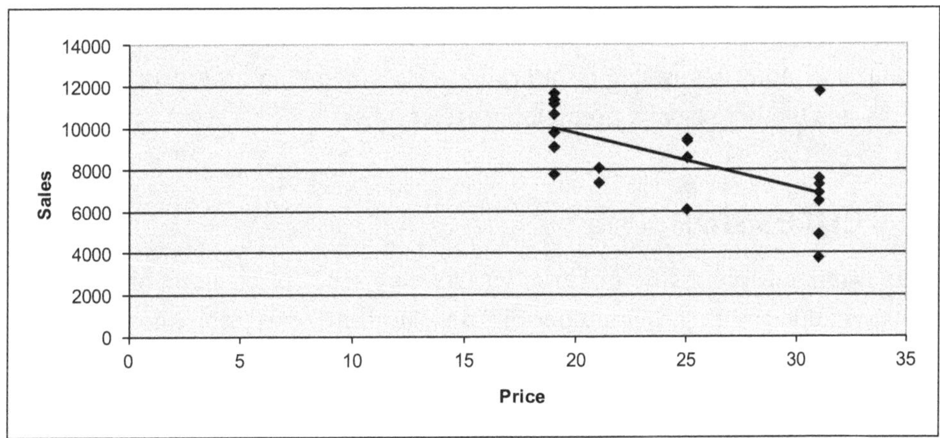

The first reason for examining the chart (put Sales, as the dependent variable/criterion, on the y axis) is to make sure that the relationship is linear. It is, with a negative correlation indicated by the left to right downward slant. The chart also shows us an outlier, another reason for examining data graphically. One coordinate is remote from the other data and is theoretically dubious: one farm is selling at the highest price and yet is also selling well. Maybe it caters for the extremely well-heeled. Let's not go there.

During data exploration, removing information just because it is inconvenient is unforgivable. However, we are now in the business of making prediction models, so it is reasonable to remove the outlier to improve the model. We are interested in generalising about what constitutes typical behaviour.

To use linear regression analysis without the outlier, *remove farm number 21 from Data View* (including the case number on the far left, to prevent the statistics package from referring to 'missing data').

The chart with just 20 cases looks more tightly knit.

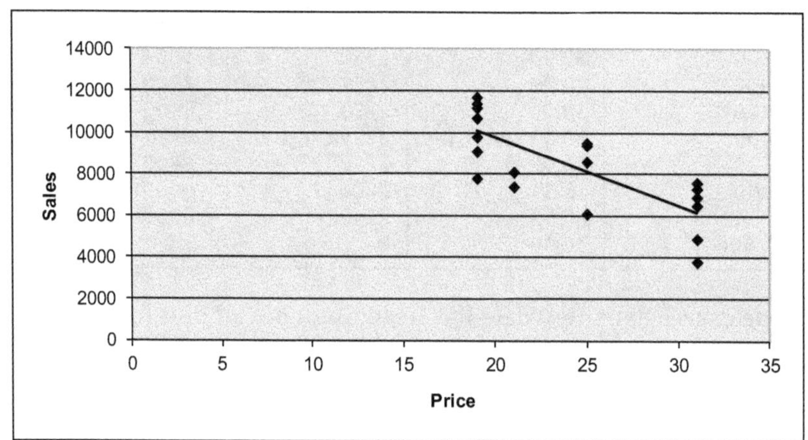

For analysis without the outlier, *Analyze/Regression/Linear.* Transfer 'Sales' to the Dependent box and 'Price' to the Independent box, ensure the method box reads 'enter', then press 'OK'.

The correlation is now –.767, which gives an effect size (*Adjusted R Square* in 'Model Summary') of .566. Considerably more of the variance is accounted for, over half, so we have a more valid predictive tool. It may now be possible to interpolate from X to Y, in other words to generalise that adjusting the price is likely to have a predictable effect on sales.

Multiple regression

Here, the focus is on multiple predictor variables. We may ask if price on its own is the only significant factor in determining the number of sales. Multiple regression allows us to build a *model* for effective prediction. We can ask two important questions. Would additional variables make an appreciable difference to predictions? And if they do, are some variables more useful than others?

DATA ENTRY

This is the same as for correlations and simple regression.

ANALYSIS

Analyze/Regression/Linear. Make Sales the 'Dependent Variable' (Y axis) – remember the outlying 21st case should have been removed – then select Price, Online marketing, Local radio and Local press as 'Independent Variables'. All of these except Price relate to advertising expenditure. Ensure the method box reads 'enter' and click 'OK'.

Coefficients[a]

Model		Unstandardized Coefficients		Standardized Coefficients	t	Sig.
		B	Std. Error	Beta		
1	(Constant)	-821.105	4592.545		-.179	.860
	Average price	-289.770	51.597	-.677	-5.616	.000
	Online marketing	.892	1.171	.098	.762	.458
	Local radio	.558	.329	.215	1.697	.110
	Local press	.849	.275	.377	3.082	.008

a. Dependent Variable: Sales numbers

The coefficients are informative: Price is significant (inversely, $r = -0.677$), as is Local press.

To find out whether or not additional variables make an appreciable difference to our predictive model, see the 'Model Summary': $R = .892$ and the effect size of .741 (*Adjusted R Square*) accounts for 74% of the variance. As the effect size of the simple regression was .566, this model is clearly more effective: we would do well to consider other factors as well as price when predicting sales.

Before going further, it may be worth checking for statistical safety. Run the regression again but this time press the 'Plots' button in order to examine the residuals:

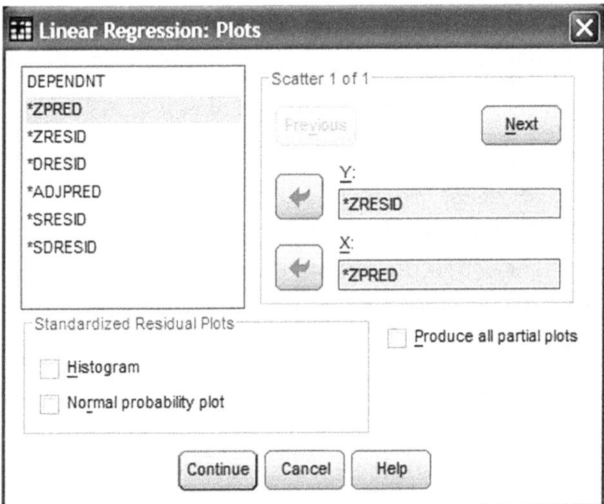

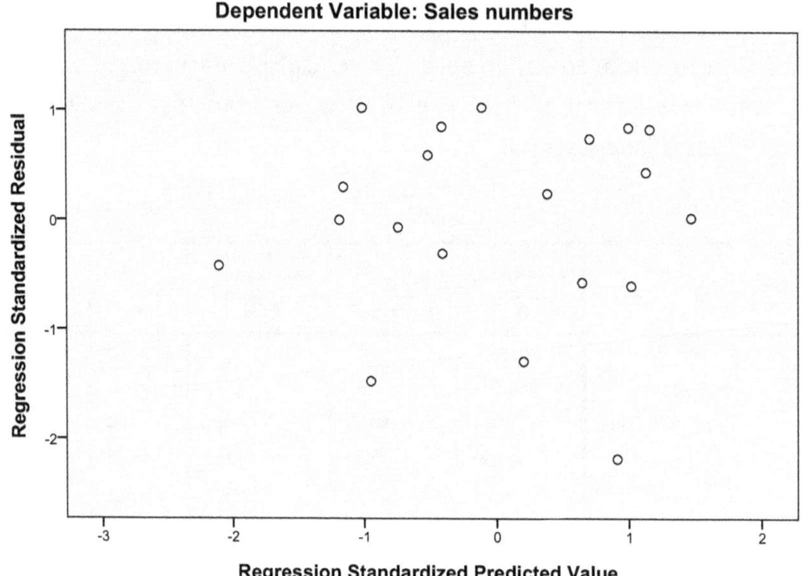

The residuals, essentially errors, are randomly spread. This is favourable.

Also calculate '*Collinearity*': essentially, high collinearity means that variables are over-correlated with each other, possibly meaning that they measure the same underlying construct; if this is the case, we would need to get rid of unnecessary variables. (Rather than fishing for results, you should only include variables that 'make sense'.) Re-run the regression calculation, this time pressing the 'Statistics' button and selecting 'Collinearity diagnostics'. Consult the Coefficients output box, where you will find Collinearity Statistics columns on the far right. A high Tolerance factor, approaching 1, is desirable; as the Tolerance column here shows figures between .821 and .939, this is good. We also want a low VIF – variance inflation factor – where not being far above 1 is good; the VIF figures here are also satisfactory, being between 1.065 and 1.218.

Returning to the significance levels, it seems worthwhile to refine our model by removing 'Online marketing' and 'Local radio' as less influential factors. So, when we go back and perform multiple regression with only 'Price' and 'Local press' as predictors, our two factors account for considerably more of the variance than the simple model.

This time, $R = .851$, with an effect size (*Adjusted R Square*) of .691, almost 70% of the variance. We do not seem to have lost much by removing the other predictor variables while gaining considerable clarity by having only two. It is always possible, however, to look for another relevant factor.

The procedure above is Standard Multiple Regression, also known as Simultaneous Multiple Regression, all variables being examined at the same time. Usually this is the only method you will need. Another method, Sequential or Hierarchical, is used when you believe that the order of variable entry is important; this is why there is a Method box in the Linear Regression dialog box. As with standard regression only more so, a theory of what is being examined is necessary for deciding what technique to use.

PARTIAL CORRELATION: 'PARTIALLING OUT'

In various reports, you will come across the idea of variables being 'controlled for'. This is useful when variables are likely to overlap each other. This sort of analysis can inform our use of regression analyses and also may help us to decide which variables to exclude in factor analyses (to be dealt with later). We are comparing the results of two diagnostic tests, as we did towards the end of the discussion of the Pearson test, but here let us control for age, statistically removing its influence.

Data entry

As with correlations and regression.

Use the 'Parallels' file, relating to two similar diagnostic tests, as used with the Pearson test. Create a new variable in *Variable View*, 'Age', adding these figures in Data View: 16, 21, 17, 16, 20, 18, 30, 22, 27, 23.

Analysis

Analyze/Correlate/Partial. Transfer Diagnostic Test A and Diagnostic Test B to the Variables box, and Age to the 'Controlling for' box. Let us assume that previous research indicates that older people will generally have higher scores on the tests, so we should opt for a one-tailed significance reading. Otherwise, we should choose the more rigorous two-tailed test. Given the small data set, it seems reasonable to set our expectations of the acceptable significance level at $p < 0.5$.

To view the means alongside the other test results, use the 'Options' button; as well as 'Means and standard deviations', select 'Zero-order correlations' to compare the controlled for results with the original (zero order) correlations. Press 'Continue' then 'OK'.

The outputs show a Correlations box. The 'zero order' correlations in the first half of the table show the coefficients without the partialling out. Each variable on the left is shown in turn, correlated with the variables listed at the top. The results which show '1.000' are of course where a variable is correlated with itself.

Here, the Pearson test ($r = .971$, $p < .0005$ one-tailed), indicates an extremely strong relationship between the results from the two tests. However, there is also a clear relationship between each of the tests and the age of the participants; even if the two-tailed test had been used and the significance readings had doubled to .024 for Test A and .016 for Test B, both would have remained significant for our purposes.

In the lower section comes the partial coefficient ($r = .942$). The strong relationship between the parallel tests still exists, so we can be confident in their reliability (unless something untoward is happening at the test venue). However, it is somewhat smaller and reduces the effect size: if we square the earlier and later coefficients for the test papers, we get $r^2 = .942$ and .887. In this case, we have a more accurate assessment, but the difference is not great. This is not always the case of course.

As suggested earlier, partialling out can assist in working out which factors to exclude in factor analysis. Before we study factor analysis, however, we need to consider multiple correlation.

THE MULTIPLE CORRELATION MATRIX

This allows us to study the pattern of relationships between more than two variables.

Data entry

As with correlations and regression. Use the 'sales' data from the multiple regression example.

Analysis

One simple way of examining multiple correlations is to transfer more than two variables in *Analyze/Correlate/Bivariate.* If you do this with data from the multiple regression exercise, you will find that the output is not very readable. However, this method does have the advantage of offering non-parametric tests (Spearman and Kendall's tau-b) as well as parametric tests.

A rather neater version can be found using *Analyze/Dimension Reduction/Factor,* but the test uses the Pearson test and is thus suited to parametric data only. Press the 'Descriptives' button and select 'coefficients' for the correlation matrix; you may also choose 'significance levels' as shown here in the lower section of the correlation matrix. (The other output can be safely ignored unless or until you read about factor analysis.)

Correlation Matrix

		Sales numbers	Average price	Online marketing
Correlation	Sales numbers	1.000	-.767	.320
	Average price	-.767	1.000	-.116
	Online marketing	.320	-.116	1.000
	Local radio	.200	.036	.363
	Local press	.534	-.229	.172
Sig. (1-tailed)	Sales numbers		.000	.085
	Average price	.000		.313
	Online marketing	.085	.313	
	Local radio	.199	.440	.058
	Local press	.008	.166	.234

Correlation Matrix

		Local radio	Local press
Correlation	Sales numbers	.200	.534
	Average price	.036	-.229
	Online marketing	.363	.172
	Local radio	1.000	-.071
	Local press	-.071	1.000
Sig. (1-tailed)	Sales numbers	.199	.008
	Average price	.440	.166
	Online marketing	.058	.234
	Local radio		.383
	Local press	.383	

Two common features of correlation matrices may be seen. Firstly, where a variable is correlated with itself, a perfect correlation (1.000) is observed. Secondly, on either side of the perfect correlations are two triangular matrices, each a mirror image. So you only need to pay attention to one of the data triangles (the lower half is probably easier to look at).

Please also note that the lower table offers a one-tailed significance reading. Unlike the bivariate correlation, it is expected with multiple correlations that you will already have some idea of what you are analysing. We will now develop this argument.

There is a danger in examining ever greater numbers of variables. The more correlations that are calculated, the greater the probability of apparently significant relationships really turning out to be chance results. If we decide on a significance level of $p < .05$ then each test has a one in twenty chance of being a fluke. (The danger of reporting fluke results as significant applies to other tests; running a large series of *t* tests in order to 'see what is significant' is a well-known error.) So 'dredging' for data, seeing what emerges from throwing a lot of variables together, is ill-advised.

One way of tackling this problem is a strictly statistical approach, raising the bar for which correlations we are willing to accept. One highly conservative method of doing this is the Bonferroni technique, simply multiplying a correlation's *p* value by the number of comparisons to get an adjusted *p* value. If we take our multiple regression example using all the variables there, we find that there are 10 pairings, 10 sets of results.

The radio promotion *p* value is $p = 0.008$, $p < .01$; with 10 comparisons, the Bonferroni gives 0.08, non-significant. This is rather harsh and – this is the real world entering our calculations – almost certainly wrong. The Bonferroni is particularly fierce when applied to a large number of tests. My own method, the number of pairings minus 0.5, still provides an insignificant result: $0.008 \times 9.5 = 0.076$. Either we invent a new, more sensitive test, or do the sensible thing: reduce the number of variables to those of genuine interest.

Let us reduce our examination to sales, price and local press, as our multiple regression recommends.

Correlation Matrix

		Sales numbers	Average price	Local press
Sig. (1-tailed)	Sales numbers		.000	.008
	Average price	.000		.166
	Local press	.008	.166	

The Bonferroni adjustment, using only three comparisons, gives an adjusted *p* value of $3 \times .008 = 0.024$, $p < .05$. If we used my slightly milder technique of multiplying by the number of conditions minus 0.5 we would multiply by 2.5 giving p = 02, also $p < .05$. (If you used this approach to adjusting significance values, you would need to report it.)

Generally, I would suggest that significance adjustment is not a suitable fix without a well-considered reduction of the number of variables.

The situation becomes even muddier when there are clearly significant correlations but with relatively small effect sizes. A coefficient of .44 for example has an effect size accounting for less than 20% of the variance. Is that significant in the everyday sense of the word? The conflict between what is statistically significant and what is meaningful is a common problem and varies according to context.

Data analysis in the real world may be less clear than in our example. As well as concerns over useful degrees of magnitude, the use of multiple correlations, with a range of sizable coefficients, may make it very difficult to 'eyeball' the correlations for meaning. Although statistical outputs rarely allow the analyst to dispense with subjective judgement, some decision-making can be assisted by exploratory factor analysis.

FACTOR ANALYSIS: A DATA REDUCTION METHODOLOGY

Explanations of factor analysis in all its diverse glory are rather difficult to absorb. This being the case, a simplified account is given here. When you get to read more detailed accounts, you will find that I have glossed over rather a lot; but if you get to read and understand such accounts, then this summary will have fulfilled its purpose.

Exploratory factor analysis

Exploratory factor analysis takes multiple correlations and extracts from them underlying variables, otherwise known as factors or dimensions. The quest for factor analytic techniques is to find what some textbooks refer to as *simple structure*, a tight and meaningful separation of factors.

In other words, the number of variables should be reduced into a smaller number of components, which hopefully will be meaningful. For example, survey respondents declare preferences over a wide range of options and you may want to find out if there are a few common attitudes which account for many of the responses. You may also want to see if there are common factors underlying a range of animal behaviours. Exploratory factor analysis may also be used in the analysis of mineral deposits, of the tissues of animals or humans, etc.

As usual, there are practical considerations. It is better to input variables that you think are likely to be relevant rather than just lumping together all possible variables from a large study.

Also note a certain tension over how inter-correlated the correlations are. Without any relationship, there will no factors in common. On the other hand, too high a correlation between two variables suggests that they measure the same thing; one of them should be removed before conducting the factor analysis. One critique of factor analysis is that it may produce statistical artefacts rather than meaningful entities. In practical terms, this can usually be resolved by a recommendation previously given in this book: have a sensible rationale for action rather than just pressing the button to see what happens.

The literature on how to conduct factor analysis is both rich and bemusing. One problem is that the term 'factor analysis' is used both as a generic term for the extraction of underlying variables from data, as discussed above, and also as a particular group of techniques. However, the following brief explanation of the three major steps provides the essentials.

Firstly, a correlation matrix is formed from the data (as described in the previous section).

Secondly, factors are extracted. These are also known as latent variables, dimensions, or core constructs. The last of these terms is a psychological idea but may still serve us well in describing the overall process: if people hold a wide range of views, it could be that these could be boiled down to some over-arching mental concepts.

Thirdly, the factors can be rotated, in order to try to find a clearer way of viewing the factors. While bivariate correlations are clearly delineated on X and Y, the immediate clustering of variables is not necessarily a meaningful one. A metaphor could be that of constellations of stars, which appear to be real formations but are in fact clustered according to the viewer's perspective, an arbitrary way of looking at the universe. Rotation is a legitimate way of adjusting the position of the factors to achieve 'simple structure'.

Our data comprises 15 rows, representing cases (individual cattle, flocks of sheep, farms or other units) and the 12 variables, A to L. The variables could be responses to different tests, averages of physical attributes, business data, etc. The aim is to find common underlying variables, ascertain how many there are, and how far each contributes to the variance.

Table 9.6

A	B	C	D	E	F	G	H	I	J	K	L
82	92	61	28	25	16	79	54	60	43	28	61
41	44	67	51	81	45	62	61	32	57	54	67
41	72	71	74	79	30	85	57	40	51	41	39
93	84	58	43	42	15	70	70	76	69	14	20
86	92	48	54	36	26	72	69	67	59	14	26
39	53	51	75	48	42	94	84	69	58	19	39
54	45	89	54	56	42	89	60	49	47	35	40
88	98	58	27	35	11	70	62	72	57	15	33
78	97	69	53	41	12	72	67	54	46	26	42
66	92	63	76	60	28	56	43	21	39	80	83
72	95	55	79	39	35	60	53	32	53	60	74
71	87	65	73	70	13	80	65	64	65	20	33
76	80	52	67	60	16	67	52	53	54	51	56
47	61	76	45	79	36	56	63	56	55	38	51
84	81	56	73	61	48	47	39	14	34	75	87

DATA ENTRY

As with correlations and regression. In Variable View, create 'Case' (or 'Observation') and the 12 variables (A, B, C, etc.). In this study, set all 'Decimals' to zero. In Data View, enter numbers 1 to 15 for Case, and the data for the variables as shown.

Three points need to be made about the raw data. There should be at least 100 observations (we have 180), although it has been suggested that a cautious interpretation may be made with over 50. There should also be 5 times as many subjects (rows) as variables, extended to between 8 and 10 rows for each column where there are less than 100 observations (this rule has been ignored here for the sake of relatively brief data entry). Also, it is helpful to place variables that you believe to be related side by side.

ANALYSIS

Analyze/Dimension Reduction/Factor. In the factor analysis dialog box, transfer the relevant variables to the Variables box on the right.

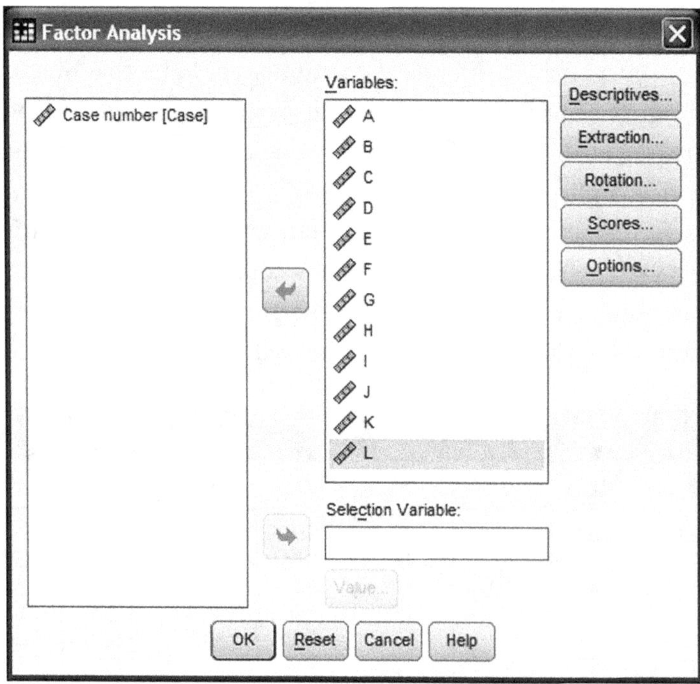

To the right of the Variables box, you will see a series of buttons. Here, we will be paying attention to 'Descriptives', 'Extraction' and 'Rotation', selecting a range of suggested settings (adapted from Kinnear and Gray 2004), which will be discussed during the SPSS output.

In 'Descriptives', select the following options: Under 'Statistics', tick both Univariate descriptives and Initial solution. Under 'Correlation Matrix', tick Coefficients, KMO and Bartlett's test of sphericity and also Reproduced. Press 'Continue'.

In 'Extraction': the 'Method' scroll bar should be set to 'Principal components'. Under 'Analyze', choose Correlation matrix. Under 'Display', select both Unrotated factor solution and Scree plot. Under 'Extract', select Based on Eigenvalue with a setting of Eigenvalues greater than: 1. Use the default setting of 25 for Maximum Iterations for Convergence. Press 'Continue'.

In 'Rotation': under 'Method', select Varimax. Under 'Display', select Rotated solution. Again, use the default setting of 25 for Maximum Iterations for Convergence. Press 'Continue'.

After all that, you can press 'OK' in the Factor Analysis dialogue box and examine the output.

The descriptive statistics for each variable comprise the mean, standard deviation and number of cases. Then comes the correlation matrix, as discussed in the multiple correlations exercise. I suggest, however, transferring the matrix data to a spreadsheet ('paste special', using text rather than an image).

	A	B	C	D	E	F	G	H	I	J	K	L
A	1											
B	0.80	1										
C	-0.46	-0.49	1									
D	-0.34	-0.09	-0.15	1								
E	-0.68	-0.59	0.45	0.40	1							
F	-0.61	-0.70	0.20	0.40	0.44	1						
G	-0.30	-0.28	0.19	-0.05	-0.17	-0.17	1					
H	-0.22	-0.27	-0.07	-0.21	-0.17	-0.15	0.64	1				
I	0.23	0.10	-0.15	-0.53	-0.42	-0.58	0.58	0.79	1			
J	-0.01	-0.10	-0.18	-0.17	0.02	-0.33	0.33	0.72	0.72	1		
K	-0.18	-0.06	0.05	0.52	0.40	0.51	-0.65	-0.83	-0.95	-0.68	1	
L	-0.10	0.01	-0.05	0.36	0.20	0.47	-0.65	-0.79	-0.88	-0.74	0.92	1

Remove the upper half of the computer-generated matrix; it is a mirror image of the lower half and can make it difficult to see what is going on. The cells here have been conditionally formatted; figures larger than 0.3 or smaller than −0.3 are in a darker font. Correlations of lesser magnitude, positive or negative, tend not to be meaningful in this context. (Users of the principal components default extraction setting should note the rule that some correlations should be larger than 0.3.)

It was previously suggested that variables which are likely to be closely inter-related should be placed in adjacent columns of the raw data. This allows easier viewing of any correlation clusters. It is always a good idea to guess which variables are closely related before analysis; as usual, there should be a rationale behind data selection. In the case of the correlation matrix, a failure to align the variables will make it more difficult to eyeball the data. When you are clear about what the data means, the nature of the factors should become clearer.

Here, we can see that variables K and L are highly correlated and have strong negative relationships with several other variables; often a construct will be partially defined by opposites. A and B are also highly correlated, with a grouping of positive relationships.

The next output item shows the KMO (Kaiser–Meyer–Olkin Measure of Sampling Adequacy) and Bartlett's test of sphericity (sphericity being a statistical assumption for repeated measures). For our input data to be suitable for a satisfactory factor analysis, the KMO statistic should be greater than .5; the small number of rows when compared to columns in this data set make it unsurprising that KMO = .320 on this occasion. The test of sphericity significance level should be smaller than .05, which it is in this case, with a p value of .000 ($p < .0005$).

The Communalities output shows how much of the variance has been accounted for by a variable. The readings here range from .598 in the case of variable G through to .968 for variable K.

Component	Initial Eigenvalues		
	Total	% of Variance	Cumulative %
1	5.280	43.996	43.996
2	3.228	26.897	70.893
3	1.200	10.004	80.897
4	.837	6.972	87.868
5	.725	6.039	93.907
6	.259	2.160	96.067
7	.184	1.532	97.600
8	.138	1.148	98.747
9	.076	.633	99.380
10	.040	.336	99.716
11	.032	.269	99.985
12	.002	.015	100.000

Extraction Method: Principal Component Analysis.

Components 1 to 12 on the left of the Total Variance Explained box (edited) are only of consequence in showing the order of size of potential components, from largest to smallest. As any components could conceivably be considered as factors, we need a way of deciding on a cut-off. As will be discussed, this can be a matter of judgement, depending on attributes known to the researcher, but the reading of Eigenvalues, shown in the Total column, is a useful statistically based cut-off procedure.

The Eigenvalue represents the total amount of variance contributed to by a factor. Usually, we use Kaiser's criterion (Kaiser 1960), which takes into account only components with Eigenvalues of 1 or more. In this case, there would appear to be three discernible factors.

Eigenvalues, however, just act as a guide, useful when the divide between potential factors is unclear. If the criterion in our example had been the meaningfulness of the potential categories, then four factors might conceivably have been considered. The number of factors in practical research should be influenced by theory and/or empirical evidence. All other things being equal, however, a theory with fewer factors is usually preferable.

In the example, factors 1, 2 and 3 are seen to account initially for 44%, 27% and 10% of the variance, accounting together for almost 81%. Rotation of the factors (the 'Rotation Sums of Squared Loadings' output) adjusts the variance estimates to 40%, 30% and 11% respectively.

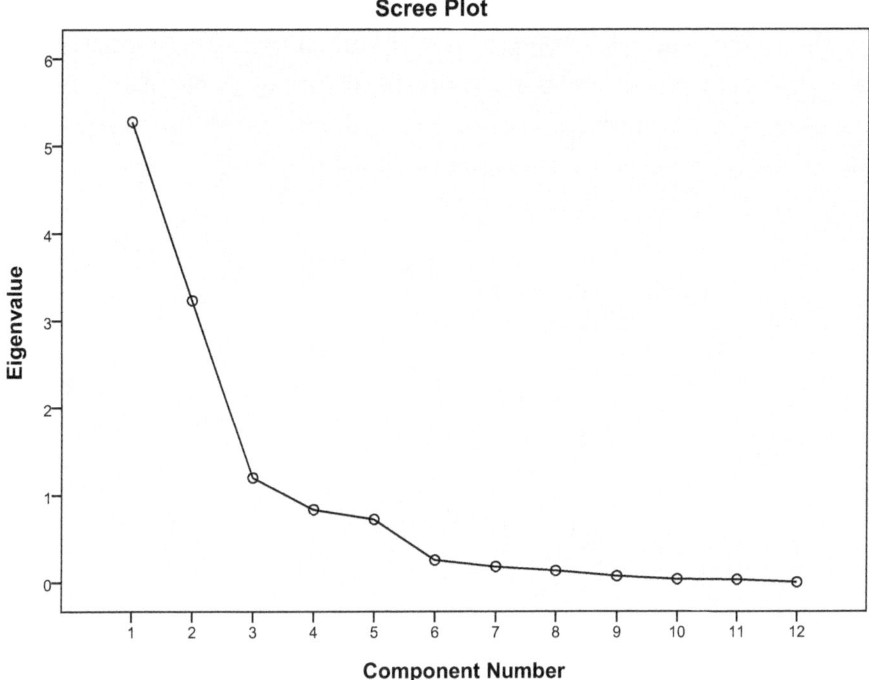

The scree plot is a traditional guide for deciding how many factors would be meaningful and is argued by some to be the best (Costello and Osborne 2005). The last point before the slope starts to level off is considered usable. Here, the plot appears to support the guidance from the Eigenvalues.

The next output item is the Component Matrix, which appears as three columns, which refer to the three components estimated by the program. Correlations between the factors and the test are called 'loadings'. A type of pattern emerges, with some variables scoring more highly in different columns, each column representing one underlying dimension. Generally, we are interested in statistics greater than 0.3 and, in negative relationships, smaller than −0.3. The figures are best transferred to a spreadsheet and conditionally formatted to highlight the groupings (some analysts prefer a 0.5 rather than a 0.3 cut-off).

	1	2	3
A	-0.29	**-0.89**	-0.06
B	-0.18	**-0.90**	0.09
C	0.16	**0.55**	**-0.72**
D	**0.51**	0.19	**0.69**
E	**0.48**	**0.63**	0.05
F	**0.63**	**0.54**	0.14
G	**-0.60**	**0.48**	0.00
H	**-0.79**	**0.46**	0.23
I	**-0.98**	0.05	-0.02
J	**-0.72**	0.27	**0.35**
K	**0.97**	-0.13	0.07
L	**0.91**	-0.24	0.01

The upper half of the 'Reproduced Correlations' output box then provides a set of 'Reproduced Correlations' related to the loadings. The lower box, 'Residual', warns that there are 25 residuals with significance values of greater than 0.05. Residuals should be as small as possible to show a good 'fit' between the original matrix and the reproduced one. So in this exercise, this is another sign that perhaps some variables are surplus to requirements.

	A	B	C	D	E	F	G	H	I	J	K	L
A		-0.05	0.03	0.02	0.03	**0.06**	-0.05	-0.03	-0.01	0.05	-0.01	-0.06
B	-0.05		**0.10**	**0.12**	**0.07**	-0.12	0.05	-0.02	-0.03	-0.02	-0.01	-0.04
C	0.03	**0.10**		**0.15**	**0.06**	-0.10	0.02	-0.02	-0.03	0.04	0.01	-0.06
D	0.02	**0.12**	**0.15**		0.00	-0.12	**0.17**	-0.04	-0.03	-0.08	0.00	-0.07
E	0.03	**0.07**	**0.06**	0.00		-0.21	-0.19	-0.09	0.02	**0.18**	0.01	-0.09
F	**0.06**	-0.12	-0.10	-0.12	-0.21		-0.04	**0.08**	0.00	-0.06	-0.05	0.03
G	-0.05	0.05	0.02	**0.17**	-0.19	-0.04		-0.05	-0.04	-0.23	0.00	0.02
H	-0.03	-0.02	-0.02	-0.04	-0.09	**0.08**	-0.05		0.00	-0.05	-0.02	0.05
I	-0.01	-0.03	-0.03	-0.03	0.02	0.00	-0.04	0.00		0.01	0.01	0.02
J	0.05	-0.02	0.04	-0.08	**0.18**	-0.06	-0.23	-0.05	0.01		0.04	-0.02
K	-0.01	-0.01	0.01	0.00	0.01	-0.05	0.00	-0.02	0.01	0.04		0.01
L	-0.06	-0.04	-0.06	-0.07	-0.09	0.03	0.02	0.05	0.02	-0.02	0.01	

A formatted spreadsheet version of the residuals, with > .05 converted to bold font, suggests that variables B and C are particularly suspect. The original correlation matrix, particularly when formatted, suggested that these variables did not correlate well with the rest of the data set.

The 'Rotated Component Matrix' provides the most clear-cut information, but it is clearest if transferred to a spreadsheet and formatted, as here. The numbers which are larger than .5 and smaller than –.5 are emphasised. This is a rather more effective cut-off than > .3 and < –.3.

	1	2	3
A	-0.096	**-0.932**	-0.011
B	-0.17	**-0.897**	0.154
C	-0.07	**0.541**	**-0.74**
D	-0.263	0.403	**0.734**
E	-0.18	**0.775**	0.055
F	-0.336	**0.748**	0.175
G	**0.732**	0.199	-0.149
H	**0.934**	0.113	0.051
I	**0.898**	-0.343	-0.173
J	**0.823**	-0.031	0.2
K	**-0.916**	0.274	0.232
L	**-0.916**	0.142	0.176

The three factors appear in sharper relief (although questions remain, at least about B and C as members of group 2).

Finally, we get to the Component Transformation Matrix, which relates to how the components have changed since rotation. Which reminds me: you should use an orthogonal rotation solution when factors are *not* expected to be highly correlated with each other; the SPSS orthogonal options are Varimax, most commonly used and the default in this example, Quartimax and Equamax. An oblique solution should be used where factors *are* expected to be highly inter-correlated; the SPSS oblique options are Direct Oblimin and Promax. (Reiley 2012 provides a short and useful internet article on rotation methods. Costello and Osborne 2005, also useful and available online, are not keen on my choice of principal components as the default extraction method.)

Generally speaking, a third factor seems likely to have explanatory power in this example. In the case of real-life variables, however, we are likely to have more of a clue as to what a factor consists of and its relative importance. Real world considerations would probably inform us whether or not smaller factors have any meaning or are merely mathematical constructs.

The above considerations lead me to say that, despite all the calculations, exploratory factor analysis is rather subjective, an art as well as a science.

One real life example is a study of ground water quality in an Iraqi plain (Shihab and Abdul Baqi 2010). The variables studied included acidity/alkalinity, calcium, magnesium, sodium, boron, potassium, and nitrate. One analysis related to 35 deep water wells, another to 28 shallow wells (each well constituting a case). The researchers found two factors pertaining to the deep wells, three factors for the shallow wells. In both sets of wells, the first factor represented more than 50% of the variance in water quality. The deep wells exhibited less variation in calcium and carbonate ions, the shallow ones less variation in potassium and nitrate. The researchers went on to use cluster analysis to classify the wells into groups and believe that the results overall could prove useful to farmers and to users of ground water in the area.

Confirmatory factor analysis

CFA is a relatively advanced technique and will not be covered in detail here. While exploratory factor analysis (EFA) looks at data in a 'bottom-up' way, attempting to create a model of underlying factors, Confirmatory Factor Analysis works 'top-down'. It uses data to confirm or test models with factors. Models can be tested against each other. A model's reliability can be tested; in the exercise, you could try out new sets of data to find out which is more useful, a two- or three-factor model, or if the entire model is misleading (there are certainly grounds for re-running our original EFA with a couple of variables removed).

One actual study evaluated a health assessment method, testing the hypothesis from an exploratory factor analysis of a two-factor structure, physical and psychosocial dimensions of health. This was conducted using an independent sample of generally healthy children and confirmed the factor structure (Hepner and Sechrest 2002).

The principal components setting was used for EFA in this book, but this is not universally favoured (Costello and Osborne 2005). In CFA, a factor analysis technique, such as principal axis factoring, is more likely to be selected from the 'Extraction' settings, with rotation methods selected according to situation and theoretical leaning (Reiley 2012). Often, CFA is part of a broader research methodology known as structural equation modelling.

DISCUSSION POINT

We have already established that apparently strong correlations may be coincidental. Do too many tests and that five-in-a-hundred fluke is increasingly likely to occur.

Another perceived weakness of correlations is that they do not prove cause and effect. This is, of course, a problem. For example, a meta-analysis of research studies provided increasing evidence of a relationship between sleeplessness and early deaths (Cappuccio *et al.* 2010). Another study (Kripke *et al.* 2012) indicated a relationship between the use of hypnotic sleeping pills and mortality. These studies suggest that insomnia or (and?) sleeping pills cause ill-health. But the logic could run counter-intuitively. Perhaps unhealthy ways of living, likely causes of terminal ill-health, may carry the side-effects of insomnia and related drug usage.

One way of sorting out the problem is to run experiments or quasi-experiments. It is not always practical to do so, however. Triangulation of methods may also be used; different aspects of a problem may be subjected to different forms of analysis to see if the original theory can be disproven. Confirmatory factor analysis, for example, could be used to test the given relationship, looking at different variables to examine the direction of an effect or to provide more explanatory models. Methods such as structural equation modelling are also used to examine the direction of correlational effects.

This proliferation of different methods of looking at the same thing reminds me of something: the General Linear Model (GLM). You may have noticed some tell-tale clues that differences and similarities examined in this book sometimes appear to be inter-related. See for example the analysis of the between-subjects three-way ANOVA and, in factorial ANOVA charts, the possibility of extrapolating as with regression lines. GLM in fact underlies factorial ANOVA, the *t* test, regression and factor analysis (which is probably enough for a book for beginner and intermediate test users).

This table of tests of relationships is not exhaustive, but refers to tests used in this chapter.

Table 9.7

N.B. *Non-parametric tests can be used with 'parametric' data.*
Do also note that non-parametric linear regression may be found on some statistical packages, for example StatsDirect.

Purpose	Number of variables	Data	Test
Correlation	2	Non-parametric	Spearman/tau-b
	2	Parametric	Pearson
	More than 2	Both possible	Multiple correlation
	2, + 1 or more controls	Parametric	Partial correlation
Prediction	2	Parametric	Linear regression
	More than 2	Parametric	Multiple regression
Data reduction	Multi-variable	Parametric	Factor analysis

PART THREE

Miscellaneous

CHAPTER 10

Exercises

QUESTIONS

Question 1

Two computer algorithms, A and B, were compared for their effectiveness over a range of the same data mining samples. For each sample, either one algorithm or the other was considered better. Of 40 such trials, Algorithm A was more successful on 26 occasions. What test should be used and what is the outcome? Accept a significance level of $p < .05$.

Question 2

Patients with the same clinical problems were randomly allocated to treatment in hospital or at home to see if the venue had any effect. After an agreed period of time, progress ratings on a five point scale were contrasted. What test is appropriate?

Question 3

Assuming a proven relationship between water levels and subsequent flooding in a given area, what method should we use to estimate likely damage?

Question 4

We are aware of evidence of ethnic and gender differences amongst patients with glaucoma (Takusagawa and Mansberger 2012). In this completely fictional follow-up we want to examine the relationship between ethnicity and gender amongst a sample of people suffering from this eye condition.

Table 10.1

	Caucasian	West Indian	African	Asian
Female	6	11	20	30
Male	8	18	16	32

What method should we use? Are there significant differences?

Question 5

Three different engineering proposals are being considered. For each proposal, we have a quantified history, with successes, failures and 'mixed results'. Engineering proposal A had 100 successes, 230 failures and 150 mixed results. Engineering proposal B had 600 successes, 400 failures and 100 mixed results. Engineering proposal C had 180 successes, 120 failures and 100 mixed results.

Consider an appropriate design and find out if the test results are significant.

Question 6

A correlation matrix containing a lot of variables includes many correlations at .9. What should you do?

Question 7

Can a correlation coefficient of .2 be significant?

ANSWERS

Answer 1

This is a dichotomous (yes or no) analysis of differences; the binomial test should be used. The 26:14 ratio would be significant with a one-tailed level of significance. But did we really have solid preconceptions about Algorithm A being superior? If not, the two-tailed level of significance is applicable. Our result is not significantly different from chance at the two-tailed level.

Answer 2

Mann–Whitney examines the differences between two different sets of individuals. (If the rating scales had been calibrated, the unpaired *t* test could have been used.)

Answer 3

Linear regression. The water level would be used to predict likely flooding.

Answer 4

Chi-square test of association. Not significant.

Answer 5

Table 10.2			
	Successes	**Failures**	**Mixed**
Proposal A	100	230	150
Proposal B	600	400	100
Proposal C	180	120	100

Chi-square. Clearly significant.

Answer 6

Analyze/Regression/Linear. Open the 'statistics' option and select 'Collinearity diagnostics'. Some variables probably have very similar meanings and should be removed. Similarities are useful, but not duplication. When your cull has lowered the collinearity of your data set, you could then use factor analysis to reduce the data further, allowing a more in-depth investigation of the correlations.

Answer 7

This sort of correlation coefficient can be quite common when dealing with large data sets and may be accompanied by an acceptable *p* value. What is more important is to work out just how useful the finding is. Is an effect size of .04 going to be significant in the everyday sense? In some cases, 4% of the variance may be important; in other cases, such an effect size is negligible in its import.

CHAPTER 11

Reporting in applied settings

This chapter is devoted to applied settings. Those preparing reports for a university or a professional body should refer to the guidelines of that particular body or to books covering your specific discipline.

RAW DATA OR CENTRAL TENDENCY?

Reporting basic data is more of a problem than you might think. Sometimes, the central tendency may make more sense; this is especially the case when comparing or contrasting rather different things, where different groups' results will be of differing sizes but the sizes are irrelevant. At other times, absolute numbers are needed; this is especially the case if the disparity of sizes in raw data is the relevant factor. Consider the following:

* Do make it clear which you are using – the central tendency or raw data – for the reader's understanding and also for your own sanity when you later try to explain what it was all about!
* When presenting nominal (categorical/qualitative) data, use the raw frequencies.
* If you do use central tendency, decide which measure to use.
* You use the mode to show the most common response.
* Use the median to reflect lumpy data, typical with non-parametric testing.
* In general, use the mean with the results from parametric tests.
* Where continuous data is 'skewed' away from normal distribution, use the median.

Again, dealing with parametrics, the mean may also be accompanied by the standard deviation (SD), a way of representing dispersion from the mean in a standardised way. SD can be positive or negative, depending upon which way it varies from the mean (SD = 0). However, before you think that you've actually found an objective way of measuring an effect, think again. The meaning of the size of the SD depends upon what you are measuring and how. You need to look at the distribution as a whole; a comparison with similar investigations, where possible, usually helps. However, the SD may be meaningful for readers who have experience of your particular area of investigation.

Where we use skewed data, the meat of non-parametric tests, then the median is more appropriate. It is not sensitive to extreme items of data.

CHARTS

When you want to create charts, especially ones where you can alter the style and what the things say, statistical packages are not particularly easy to use. Spreadsheets such as Microsoft Excel are generally a better option.

Of the available charts, pie charts are particularly useful for comparing nominal data; data must be exclusive, everything falling into one category or another. For clear contrasts, consider using columns. However, you may prefer bar charts when you have several categories, as you can let your chart stretch down the page with variable names at the side.

Spreadsheets can also be used to create simple correlation charts. In Excel, you can supplement this from the Chart menu, using 'Add Trendline'.

More complex graphs are also available, for example with different layers lying on top of one another. If you make use of these, explain carefully what the charts are saying. When I see these in newspapers, I am not always sure what is being portrayed.

WRITTEN REPORTING

For the applied researcher, readers of research are likely to be at one of three levels of sophistication. The sophisticated reader will be well acquainted with statistical methods. The intermediate reader will probably remember such things as the nature of correlations and levels of significance. The unsophisticated reader will be unfamiliar with *p* values, for example, and is unlikely to recognise the difference between 'significant' in its statistical sense and its everyday definition of meaningfulness.

I will concern myself here with statistical concepts which might or might not be included in a report to some extent. The decision-making will be dependent upon the audience, based upon the level of reader you believe you are dealing with.

Significance

In any case, except for the most academically inclined of sophisticated readers, you will omit the null hypothesis. The lay reader will generally be unconcerned with this and may even be confused by the apparent paradox of wanting to reject a hypothesis in order to prove one. It should be enough to report that a result is 'significant' or 'non-significant'. Relatively sophisticated readers will want to know the level of significance (e.g. $p = .023$ or significant to level $p < .05$), although it should be explained to intermediate level readers, at least when you first introduce levels, that this refers to the probability of results being chance, in this case the likelihood of a fluke being five in a hundred. Only sophisticated readers will want or need to read about 'one-tailed' or 'two-tailed' hypotheses; even for such an audience, a discussion of whether or not the effect was expected should prove helpful.

Effect size

Also grounded in the context of your research is the concept of effect size. Terms such as variance are only for sophisticated readers. The intermediate reader should be perfectly happy with 'large', 'medium-sized' or 'small' effects; you will certainly not want to refer to r^2 or other representative statistics. Be even more sparing with unsophisticated audiences: it should be enough to refer to particularly large (or small) effects.

The tests

Only sophisticated readers will want to know on a regular basis which statistical tests were being used. With the intermediate reader, you may occasionally cite Mann–Whitney, for example, but they should lightly embedded like so – 'the result was significant to $p < .05$ (Mann–Whitney)' – just to show you know what you are doing. In the case of the completely unsophisticated reader, I would omit it altogether.

Data collection

Most readers outside academic research will not be interested in exactly how you organised your data (unless it is very relevant to the project or the audience). Do of course record what you have done for the purposes of replication. The sophisticated reader will want to know about the removal of outlying data, as they will understand whether or not this is relevant.

Relevance

The main point is to provide the reader with results which are relevant to the purpose of the project. Generally, it should not read like an academic discourse, should be quite short and, while not necessarily affording entertainment, should be readable and cogent.

Mixed levels

If you are fairly sure that your audience is highly variegated, and you believe that it is important that the lower level reader is not to feel like a lemon (or whichever is your least favoured fruit), then stratify your report. Perhaps put your most basic comment as the main part of your subject, followed by a more sophisticated comment in parentheses, e.g. 'There was a significant difference between crops treated with Agent Red and those treated with Agent Mauve ($p < .05$ two-tailed). If you know that you have even more fanatical stats-hounds in the audience, then consider footnotes.

VERBAL REPORTING

The content for verbal reporting needs to be even more limited than that for written reporting. People generally do not listen long to continuous talk. Follow the previous recommendations, but also think about the following ways to stop information overload and boredom.

* Try showing one idea at a time, with a chart and maybe the relevant statistic (with your audience in mind), on one page.
* If you use slide-show presentations, try to keep it interesting. At least have sentences sliding in from the side. Avoid large slabs of text if possible.
* Many people use patterns and different colours. I think that these tend to distract audiences and reduce readability. Black and white is more effective than you might think. Try to use the same format throughout.

Whereas a written report includes connecting words, phrases or sentences to help your narrative flow, you do not want these in a graphical representation. The screenshot does not have to be grammatically correct (although the accompanying voice needs to be):

* significant difference between Agent Crimson and Agent Scarlet
* large effect size
* limitations in available data
* implications for research into blue-coded agents.

You then provide a commentary as you read from the screen – 'We found a significant difference ...' – including things of interest. 'The lack of data relating to Plants X and Y raises the question of how far this study can be generalised beyond vegetation from this part of the world.' 'While this clearly raises serious questions about the relative effectiveness of red-coded agents, it remains to be seen how blue-coded agents will react in such an environment. Further research may prove profitable in that area.'

It is a good idea to prepare your additional comments. At least do it in your head. Listeners are usually not impressed by presenters who just read off what is written on the screen. Unsurprisingly, they may think that they could have done this themselves without having to turn up and listen to you.

To have things running smoothly and to avoid stage fright, relatively inexperienced presenters may find it useful to rehearse once or twice, preferably in front of sympathetic colleagues. Address your audience, even in rehearsals, and be professional. This will increase the likelihood of your going into 'auto' mode during the real thing, unselfconsciously making the comments that you want to make.

It is not necessary to learn your words by heart. Remembering the few additional things you most want to add and mentally associating them with the key phrases should help things to run smoothly. (And if it is your first time, do not dwell on the fact: most of your audience will either have had the same experience or will have to do the same in the near future.)

DISCUSSION POINT

The key to writing good reports is to categorise things clearly, to put them in a sensible order and to omit those things which are likely to confuse or bore unnecessarily. If you are unable to omit certain tedious things, then find a place to put them where they are accessible if needed but avoidable.

While clear categorisation and knowing what to omit are core features in writing effective reports, there is a dark side to such an art. Painting a clear portrait is clearly helpful, but can amount to over-simplification. Playing to the audience can affect objectivity: there can be a tension between the audience's needs and the facts in all their balanced glory. A maxim in UK policy research (around 2006) suggested that, in some cases, researchers do not so much help to develop evidence-based policy as produce policy-based evidence. May your ideals go with you ...

CHAPTER 12

Advanced statistical techniques: a taster

While this book is primarily for beginners and intermediate users of statistical tests, a lot of research can be conducted with the methods described in this book. This chapter just provides a taste of some other, rather advanced, methods. To avoid possible confusion, I will consider only a few types of test, building upon what you have already learned.

MANOVA

A multivariate analysis of variance examines more than one criterion (dependent variable) at a time. Criteria may be affected by predictors in different ways, and may be affected by the interaction of such predictors. Criteria may or may not be clearly related.

Let us say that people with different types of hearing loss test out a new hearing aid. They rate the hearing aid using two separate quality measures, clarity and adaptability to different settings. We would want to know if each type of hearing loss leads to different views of both ratings or would the attitude to only one of these measures be different dependent on the type of sensory impairment.

CLUSTER ANALYSIS

Factor analysis, which we read about earlier, focuses on columns of data in a correlation matrix, the variables, investigating them for underlying dimensions. In surveys, for example, you may want to find out if particular core attitudes underlie a range of responses.

Cluster analysis is also a data reduction technique, but focuses on the *rows* of the matrix. Here the data is reduced to collections of cases; these can be groups of participants, subjects or objects. Within the data, can underlying groups be found which react in a different way from each other?

Here are a few examples of potential uses of cluster analysis. Within genetics, you could look for groupings of functionally related genes. In biology, you could describe communities of organisms. An artificial intelligence example could be identifying different niches within an evolutionary algorithm.

LOGISTIC REGRESSION

Research data frequently includes binary data: symptoms present and absent, male and female, success and failure, etc. We have seen useful methods for dealing with categorical (or qualitative) data in isolation – in the chapter on the frequency of observations – and we have also seen them as independent variables/predictors (e.g. as *t* test categories). Logistic regression, however, can examine binary data when it appears as the *dependent variable (criterion)*. This is particularly useful when you encounter rich data sets with both binary and measurable data. One example would be to assess whether or not tadpoles are deformed or not at sites with differing levels of selenium (Schwarz 2011). The status of the tadpoles would be the binary criterion. The levels of selenium – high, medium, low or control – would constitute the (ordinal) predictor.

COX'S REGRESSION (AKA THE COX MODEL)

This variant of survival analysis allows the researcher to take into account different factors which have a bearing on the time until an event. This may provide more accuracy than the Kaplan–Meier function, but certain statistical assumptions must be met before it can be safely used.

If we returned to our study of wave generation mechanisms, using Cox instead of the Kaplan–Meier function, we could find out if the wind and/or rain affected the results.

SOME THOUGHTS ON ANCOVA

We have touched on the analysis of covariance before. Factorial ANOVA in SPSS contains a box for *covariates*, variables which have a linear relationship with the dependent variable. In the chapter on correlations, we briefly looked at partialling out (or controlling for) a variable with a close relationship to the variables being analysed.

ANCOVA, the analysis of covariance, can be used to reduce error variance. In the analysis of different types of tennis racket, it may be that air pressure has fluctuated between trials. The air pressure would be the covariate to be controlled for.

The technique is also used to try to remove the effects of fixed groups (e.g. males and females) from a more general effect being studied.

Before using that convenient covariate box on the ANOVA dialog box, it is well worth considering some serious methodological issues.

Statistical assumptions for ANCOVA

Several statistical assumptions must be satisfied. Firstly, the same assumptions apply as for ANOVA and other parametric tests: continuous data, normal distribution and, where the number of subjects in each condition is different, homogeneity of variance. In within-subjects (repeated measures) experiments, sphericity is also considered important.

There are also specific assumptions relating to ANCOVA. An unsurprising condition is the need for the covariate to correlate with the dependent variable in a linear manner; the stronger the relationship, the more useful ANCOVA will be. This can be examined with a scatter plot.

At the same time, the variable and covariate must not be over-correlated. (The princess and the pea, or possibly Goldilocks and the bear family come to mind.) When different groups are being studied, you would need to look at the regression lines for the covariate across the different groups. The lines should run parallel to each other, neither crossing nor too close to each other. This 'homogeneity of regression', also checkable with scatter plots, is arguably the most important of the assumptions.

The covariate should be unrelated to the independent variable. This should be checked at the design stage.

If there is more than one covariate, the covariates should not be over correlated with each other. This may be checked by scatter plots and correlations.

The dangers of ANCOVA

The statistical assumptions indicate the need for a very narrowly defined data set. The proponents of ANOVA and other parametric tests often refer to their robustness. In the case of ANCOVA, evidence suggests that ANCOVA is not robust. Unreliable data may produce distortions which render interpretation difficult; misleading results have seriously flawed studies by reputable researchers (see Campbell 1989 and Buser 1995 for examples).

It is also possible that you will not encounter data which justifies using ANCOVA, which has a host of restrictions for data sets. It can also be argued that statistical control for groups is unnecessary when the restrictions already constrain them to fairly similar regression slopes.

Even when the data is correctly used, inference is difficult. There are serious critiques of the use of ANCOVA, both relating to data unreliability and the smoothing out of differences between fixed groups (Campbell 1989; Buser 1995; Miller and Chapman 2001). I would respectfully suggest that even advanced users of statistical tests should think long and hard before using ANCOVA.

Alternatives to ANCOVA

Various alternatives are possible, of which I cite the most accessible:

It is possible to use ANOVA and *t* tests without using the covariate box and accepting that the ideal has not been reached (I would still prefer this to a totally wrong result); you would record the likely existence of a mediating factor.

You could also stratify, breaking up the statistics according to groupings of different levels of the covariate (e.g. bandings of different air pressures). The categories would then be used as 'fixed factors'.

Another possibility is re-examining your model with multiple regression. Instead of using the standard regression method ('Enter' in the method box), you would use hierarchical (sequential) regression, selecting 'Stepwise'.

DISCUSSION POINT

This book does not cover all of the useful tests available to researchers. Many researchers, however, rarely climb higher than the statistical foothills, often recording central tendency and absolute data, occasionally analysing a difference or testing for a relationship.

If you have a firm grip on what you have learned in this book, which I hope was enjoyable and useful, you may not need more. However, the skills that you have acquired in working your way through it should allow you to benefit from more advanced reading and training as and when necessary.

References

Armitage P, Berry G (1994) *Statistical Methods in Medical Research.* Blackwell, Oxford.

Arndt S, Turvey C, Andreasen N (1999) Correlating and predicting psychiatric symptom ratings: Spearman's *r* versus Kendall's tau correlation. *Journal of Psychiatric Research* **33**(2), 97–104. doi:10.1016/S0022-3956(98)90046-2

Assembly of Life Sciences (1981) 'Techniques for the study of primate population ecology'. Committee on Nonhuman Primates, Subcommittee on Conservation of Natural Populations, Washington D.C.

Bakalar N (2003) *Where the Germs Are – A Scientific Safari.* John Wiley, Hoboken, NJ.

Bland M (2000) *An Introduction to Medical Statistics.* 3rd edn. Oxford University Press, Oxford.

Buser K (1995) Dangers in using ANCOVA to evaluate special education program effects. At *Annual meeting of the American Educational Research Association.* 18–22 April, San Francisco, CA. Educational Resources Center, <www.eric.ed.gov>.

Campbell K (1989) Dangers in using analysis of covariance procedures. At *Annual meeting of the Mid–South Educational Research Association.* 9–11 November, Louisville, KY. Educational Resources Center, <www.eric.ed.gov>.

Cappuccio F, D'Elia L, Strazzullo P, Miller M (2010) Sleep duration and all-cause mortality: a systematic review and meta-analysis of prospective studies. *Sleep* **33**(5), 585–592.

Clark-Carter D (1997) *Doing Quantitative Psychological Research: From Design to Report.* Psychology Press, Hove.

Costello A, Osborne J (2005) Best practice in exploratory factor analysis: four recommendations for getting the most from your analysis. *Practical Assessment Research & Evaluation* **10**(7), <http://pareonline.net/pdf/v10n7.pdf>.

Court J, Webb Ware J, Hides S (Eds) (2010) *Sheep Farming for Meat and Wool.* CSIRO PUBLISHING, Melbourne.

Dallal G (2001) *Multiple comparison procedures.* <www.jerrydallal.com/LHSP/mc.htm>.

Davis C (2010) *Statistical Testing in Practice with StatsDirect.* Llumina Press, Tamarac, FL.

Ellery Mayence C, Marshall D, Godfree R (2010) Hydrologic and mechanical control for an invasive wetland plant, *Juncus ingens*, and implications for rehabilitating and managing Murray River floodplain wetlands, Australia. *Wetlands Ecology and Management* **18**(6), 717–730. doi:10.1007/s11273-010-9191-1

Field A (2009) *Discovering Statistics Using SPSS.* Sage, London.

Fisher R (1935) *The Design of Experiments.* Oliver and Boyd, Edinburgh.

Games P (1971) Multiple comparison of means. *American Educational Research Journal* **8**(3), 531–565.

Griffin L (2007) Historical sociology, narrative and event-structure analysis: fifteen years later. *Sociologica* **3**, 1–17.

Hepner K, Sechrest L (2002) Confirmatory factor analysis of the Child Health Questionnaire–Parent Form 50 in a predominantly minority sample. *Quality of Life Research* **11**, 763–773. doi:10.1023/A:1020822518857

Hilton A, Armstrong R (2006) Stat note 6: post hoc ANOVA tests. *Microbiologist* September, <http://eprints.aston.ac.uk/9317/1/Statnote_6.pdf>.

Howell D (2011) Multiple comparisons with repeated measures. <www.uvm.edu/~dhowell/StatPages/More_Stuff/RepMeasMultComp/RepMeasMultComp.html>.

Kahneman D (2011) *Thinking, Fast and Slow.* Allen Lane, London.

Kaiser H (1960) The application of electronic computers to factor analysis. *Educational and Psychological Measurement* **20**, 141–151. doi:10.1177/001316446002000116

Kinnear P, Gray C (2004) *SPSS 12 Made Simple.* Psychology Press, Hove.

Kleinbaum D, Kupper L, Nizam A, Muller K (2008) *Applied Regression Analysis and Other Multivariable Methods.* Duxbury Press, Pacific Grove, CA.

Kripke D, Langer, R, Kline, L (2012) Hypnotics' association with mortality or cancer: a matched cohort study. *BMJ Open* **2**, e000850. doi:10.1136/bmjopen-2012-000850

McCarthy N (2009) *Engineering – A Beginners Guide.* Oneworld, Oxford.

Mendel G (1866) Versuche über Pflanzenhybriden Verhandlungen des naturforschenden Vereines in Brünn, Bd. IV für das Jahr, 1865 Abhandlungen: 3–47. A translation by Druery C and Bateson W (1901), 'Experiments in plant hybridization' (read at the Brünn Natural History Society 1865), *Journal of the Royal Horticultural Society* **26**, 1–32 can be found at <http://www.esp.org/foundations/genetics/classical/gm-65.pdf>.

Miller G, Chapman J (2001) Misunderstanding analysis of covariance. *Journal of Abnormal Psychology* **110**(1), 40–48. doi:10.1037/0021-843X.110.1.40

Parker R (1979) *Introductory Statistics for Biology.* Edward Arnold, London.

Perrigot R, Cliquet G, Mesbah M (2004) Possible applications of survival analysis in franchising research. *International Review of Retail, Distribution and Consumer Research* **14**, 129–143. doi:10.1080/0959396032000154338

Quinn G, Shin C, Maguire M, Stone R (1999) Myopia and ambient lighting at night. *Nature* **399**, 113–114. doi:10.1038/20094

Raosoft Inc. (2004) Sample size calculator. <http://www.raosoft.com/samplesize.html>.

Reiley B (2012) *Factor Analysis Rotation Methods.* <http://www.ehow.com/list_7450638_factor-analysis-rotation-methods.html>.

Rice W (1989) Analyzing tables of statistical tests. *Evolution* **43**, 223–225. doi:10.2307/2409177

Roscoe J (1975) *Fundamental Research Statistics for the Behavioral Sciences.* Holt, Rinehart and Winston, NY.

Sato T (1996) Type 1 and type 2 errors in multiple comparisons. *The Journal of Psychology* **130**(3), 293–302. doi:10.1080/00223980.1996.9915010

Schwarz C (2011) *Sampling, regression, experimental design and analysis for environmental scientists, biologists, and resource managers.* Simon Fraser University, British Columbia, <www.stat.sfu.ca/~cschwarz/Stat-650/Notes/PDF/Chapter15.pdf>.

Shihab A, Abdul Baqi Y (2010) Multivariate analysis of ground water quality of Makhmor Plain/ North Iraq. *Damascus University Journal* **26**(1), 19–26.

SSTARS (2011) *Pairwise comparisons in SAS and SPSS.* University of Kentucky, <www.uky.edu/ComputingCenter/SSTARS/www/documentation/MultipleComparisons_3.htm>.

Takusagawa H, Mansberger S (2012) Do ethnicity and gender influence glaucoma prevalence? *Ophthalmology Management* **16**, 24–28.

Tsoumakas G, Lefteris A, Vlahavas I (2005) Selective fusion of heterogeneous classifiers. *Selective Data Analysis* **9**, 511–525.

Williams E, Matheson A, Harwood C (2002) *Experimental Design and Analysis for Tree Improvement.* CSIRO PUBLISHING, Melbourne.

Yerkes R, Dodson J (1908) The relation of strength of stimulus to rapidity of habit-formation. *The Journal of Comparative Neurology and Psychology* **18**, 459–482. doi:10.1002/cne.920180503

Zadnik K, Jones L, Irvin B, Kleinstein R, Manny R, Shin J, Mutti D (2000) Myopia and ambient night-time lighting. *Nature* **404**, 143–144. doi:10.1038/35004661

Index

www.ingramcontent.com/pod-product-compliance
Lightning Source LLC
LaVergne TN
LVHW061245100826
845148LV00008B/1031

9780643107106